PEOPLE

PEOPLE

IS REAL CHANGE POSSIBLE?

GREG RUEDIGER

People

Copyright @2021 by Greg Ruediger

All rights reserved. No part of this book may be reproduced in any form or by any electronic or mechanical means, including information storage and retrieval systems, without permission in writing from the publisher, except by reviewers, who may quote brief passages in a review.

This publication contains the opinions and ideas of its author. It is intended to provide helpful and informative material on the subjects addressed in the publication. The author and publisher specifically disclaim all responsibility for any liability, loss or risk, personal or otherwise, which is incurred as a consequence, directly or indirectly, of the use and application of any of the contents of this book.

WORKBOOK PRESS LLC
187 E Warm Springs Rd,
Suite B285, Las Vegas, NV 89119, USA

Website:	https://workbookpress.com/
Hotline:	1-888-818-4856
Email:	admin@workbookpress.com

Ordering Information:
Quantity sales. Special discounts are available on quantity purchases by corporations, associations, and others. For details, contact the publisher at the address above.

ISBN-13:	978-1-957618-06-7 (Paperback Version)
	978-1-957618-07-4 (Digital Version)

REV. DATE: 1.24.2022

To Beckie

ACKNOWLEDGMENTS

The author would like to acknowledge those who participated in shaping the book. Special recognition is given to Leora Louise Jones and Joshua P. Smith. Additionally, all children and adults known and unknown whom he has directly or indirectly interacted with are recognized.

CONTENTS

Introduction 11
The Argument: Why Broad Societal Changes
Do Not Occur 16
Indoctrination: Emotions Impact on Life 40
Communication: The Medium of Emotion 71
The Impact of Emotion on Human Dignity 98
Emotion and Human Talent 121
Emotion's Impact on Policy Development and
Implementation 149
Emotion's Impact on Behavior 172
Ideas to Promote Broad Societal Change 190
Determining the Emphasis Placed on Other's
Viewpoints Questionnaire 204
Observation Form 211
Journal Template 217
References 221

INTRODUCTION

The impetus for this book was based on the ongoing desire to understand why broad societal changes do not occur. This question surfaced as a teenager when certain classmates gained opportunities when others did not. It was never more evident then in athletics. For instance, if a prominent community member stood in the corner of the gymnasium or sat in the bleachers watching practice, his son was more likely to play on Friday night. I often wondered why that happened and if that is how it has always been. If so, is that the real reason why broad societal changes do not occur? As time passed, many adults suggested reading a particular book to uncover the answer to this question. Their idea made sense at that time, but perhaps they simply masked their discomfort with my ongoing quest to understand why things are the way they are. Regardless of their intent, I began to read a vast array of books ranging from religion to economics. Many philosophies and theories were uncovered; however, after years of curiosity-led thought and study, limited answers seem to exist as to why broad societal changes do not occur. So rather than continuing to read what others might think, it was time to write my own ideas in response to this important question.

To begin, a number of caveats are needed. First, the content of the book is not based on a series of scientific studies but rather is a collection of observations from the activities of daily living. Various scholarly works, though, are included that support the author's viewpoint. The reader is reminded as well that all phenomena are shaped by a multitude of variables in an evolving context. Therefore, it is impossible to draw casual relationships between any two variables. It is also vital not to overgeneralize the observations of the writer; rather, his intent is to provide a stimulus for thought for others to consider their life experiences. With these thoughts in mind, the writing of this book, as most acts, is self-serving in spite of the altruistic notion that it may perhaps help someone else. All simplistic ideas, writing errors, and what might be perceived as narcissistic thoughts are the sole responsibility of the author.

The book is divided into two parts. The first three chapters describe how emotion more so than intellect is the reason why broad societal changes do not occur. In Chapter 1, emotion is defined as complex layers of processes that are in constant contact with the environment. At a minimum, these interactions include cognitive stimuli appraisal or evaluation of meaning and physical changes such as endocrine, autonomic, and cardiovascular. Emotion is the energy that drives, organizes, amplifies, and attenuates cognitive activity within the socially influenced, value-appraising process of the brain (Siegel, 1999). These internal sensations range from primitive reflexes and responses to multifaceted complexities described and labeled as happiness, anger, joy, sadness, guilt, fear, hope, and love. Emotion, as one would naturally expect, is reflected in someone's hopes, dreams, desires, and problems. This characteristic of the human experience surfaces, develops, and is disseminated within an indoctrination process. Chapter 2 explores this feature of life.

Indoctrination is thought of as instilling ideas and attitudes in others that are universally accepted regardless of evidence to the contrary or the absence of any proof (Arthur, 2003). If indoctrination is the promotion of a single unassailable view, education is the opposite. Education promotes the exploration of alternative viewpoints, the critical application of data and argument, and the development of skills and dispositions necessary to act on the information. Assuming that this differentiation between indoctrination and education is accurate, emotion is the logical reason as to why most adults rely on traditional beliefs rather than science to guide their thoughts and actions. Chapter 3 examines this belief by exploring how emotion shapes the content and way in which individuals and groups communicate. Six specific communication components are discussed: (1) thoughts and ideas, (2) word selection, (3) nonverbal messages, (4) listening, (5) memory, and (6) recall and use.

The second part of the book explores how emotion impacts certain aspects of life. Chapter 4 examines emotion and human dignity. Throughout time, emotion-based actions reflect how specific individuals and groups have been denied the full range of human possibility that exists within a society and culture. All the roles, places, and stereotypes forced upon them remove dignity by defining the person within frameworks that are less than or opposed to the status of full adulthood (Grygier, 1954). Today, as less obvious and more subtle forms of oppression surface and evolve, many adults continue to struggle with a lack of contentment, often feeling they have limited control in their life. As these unsettling feelings arise, fluctuate, and often persist, human talent is impacted. Chapter 5 discusses how emotion not only promotes human talent but may also hinder its recognition and growth. Variations of basic survival instincts naturally act as the foundation for the possibility of learning. Emotion, more so than intellect, then determines the energy available for children and adults to nurture their abilities. As this feature of the human experience unfolds, someone's talent does not develop in isolation or within a vacuum but rather is shaped by experiences within families, schools, and information from the media. From a broader societal perspective, policies and procedures also reflect individual and collective talents.

Chapter 6 explores emotion and policy development and implementation. It begins by examining the context and communication patterns of those developing policies. Lasswell's (1971) seven general policy questions are then used as the framework to explore how emotion has led to increased voting opportunities, religious participation, and access to public and private institutions. In spite of the significant role of emotion in decision making, many individuals still do not seem to realize its impact on the activities of daily living. Chapter 7 addresses this issue by examining behavioral norms. The emotions generated and associated with certain experiences within families, places of worship, and schools along with information gained from the media typically determine how children and adults respond to environmental stimuli. More specifically, an individual's sense of fear, shame, and guilt to some degree influences what is thought of as acceptable and unacceptable behavior. These intense feelings perhaps explain why clear behavioral norms and expectations do not seem to exist for most activities of daily living.

In Chapter 8, self-awareness is presented as the answer to promote broad societal change. Self-awareness is thought of as understanding how one's emotion and intellect affect thoughts and actions. Five specific ideas are presented to help those interested in increasing their self-awareness. They include attempting to gain an increased understanding of emotion, exploring how tradition impacts the activities of daily living, lessening concern as to what others might think, adopting a learning opportunity life perspective, and a strategy to measure self-awareness. Ideally, if enough children and adults increase their self-awareness, collective energy might become available to promote broad societal change. If not, emotion more so than intellect, will continue to lessen the likelihood of broad societal change.

THE ARGUMENT: WHY BROAD SOCIETAL CHANGES DO NOT OCCUR

Throughout time, people have starved to death, killed each other, and not profited from past experiences. Today, this pattern of behavior continues as many neighboring countries are still unable to coexist in harmony, and children have to die before a light is placed at a busy highway intersection in spite of many adults knowing that traffic difficulties were present. Why is this? Why do broad societal changes not occur? Broad societal changes do not happen because the core of human beings, emotion and intellect, is impossible to significantly alter. Emotion more so than intellect ultimately influences and determines what individuals hear, view, and do. Human existence then is simply a part of an evolutionary process in which someone is born, has certain experiences, and then they die and others take their place. Individuals therefore are merely temporary placeholders receiving and giving to others and the environment, and then they die for a new person to begin the journey of life. This life cycle continues much like how the wind blows or the ocean tides flow.

A CLARIFICATION: UNDERSTANDING THE PERSPECTIVE

A few thoughts are needed to clarify the ideas regarding emotion, intellect, and broad societal changes. Human emotions are sensations that naturally occur within a person. They range from primitive reflexes and responses to multifaceted complexities labeled and described as happiness, anger, joy, sadness, guilt, hope, love, and a variety of other terms. These internal feelings vary for each individual and present themselves on a frequency and intensity continuum. For example, when an individual has an experience, visual and auditory stimuli trigger to some degree a biological-based response. Initially, this process is reflected in a baby's cry for comfort and ultimately ends at the mourning of life. In between these periods of time, varying degrees of emotion are present in each experience. It is also apparent that verbal and nonverbal communication patterns are the mediums that articulate human emotion. The most primitive or basic example is a person's voice tone and the intensity associated with a given message (whisper/yell) . On the opposite end of the emotional spectrum are art forms that capture human feelings through song lyrics, poetry, paintings, and other means of expression. Despite the vast array of human intelligence, emotion-led behavior appears everywhere as a societal constant.

Advancements in technology have changed daily experiences. Children and adults, for instance, no longer have to walk for miles to locate a river or stream to wash their clothes as water and electricity are readily available in most homes. Other innovations, such as automobiles, refrigeration, telephones, microwave ovens, and computers, have made life easier; however, they have not significantly altered the emotional and intellectual traits of people. People are as they always have been. Many adults as well seem to experience an ongoing level of emotional insecurity that causes them to feel they have been a victim of something in life. In many cases, parents, relatives, communities, poverty, schools, and drugs are blamed for discomfort and pain. With this frame of reference, the emotional and intellectual traits of human beings is virtually impossible to significantly alter despite the many efforts of Benjamin Franklin, Eli Whitney, Thomas Edison, Mother Teresa, Martin Luther King, Bill Gates, and others who have impacted the human experience. It is also clear that no matter what future invention lies ahead, human behavior will simply reflect "people being people." People will continue to harm others, certain groups will not live in harmony resulting in wars that kill thousands, children will starve to death, and many adults will continue to spend their life attempting to improve the human condition. Some may experience success on an individual relationship level, but not on a broad societal scale.

EVERYBODY HAS A STORY, A PROBLEM, AND HAS BEEN A VICTIM OF SOMETHING

As life's journey begins and ultimately ends, genetics and socialization impact every experience. Genetics provides the foundation for who we are and who we become. No two individuals, however, possess the same emotional traits or intellectual level. With this undeniable varying biological composition, socialization processes create the narrative of one's life story. Socialization is the naturally occurring human indoctrination process that begins at birth when parents select the name of their child and the color of clothing they wear. It continues throughout time as children and adults are conditioned to believe certain information without question or evidence to the contrary. As this aspect of the human experience unfolds, characteristics of life will not change because the emotional and intellectual abilities of human beings cannot be significantly altered. Individuals should therefore place more emphasis on living in the moment rather than expending large amounts of energy reflecting upon the past or planning for the future.

SOCIALIZATION: SHAPING THE STORY

The socialization process disseminates information from one generation to the next. This natural course of action provides order and a sense of safety while shaping individual and collective identities. Unfortunately though, the emotions related to certain experiences sometimes result in simplistic thoughts and ideas. For instance, in some parts of the United States, it is believed that the problems of youth would be solved if you follow the biblical reference, "Spare the rod, spoil the child." Another example is related to families gathering each day at the dinner table. Magically, the world would be a better place when people eat together. Is that true or just emotion talking? An interesting thought though is what happens when adults reflect on the many family meals together but do not remember any discussion that substantively impacted their life? A review of other contemporary issues related to family, places of worship, school, and media (agents of emotion) might be helpful to illuminate and explain why broad societal changes do not occur.

FAMILY

Single-parent households and blended and extended families are mirrors of emotion-led behavior that fall under the category of family. In most industrialized societies, citizens accept and support the idea of escaping discomfort and pain through divorce. As these changes in thinking continue to evolve, many parents seem to act as though they are peers of their children rather than adults. Why is this? The simple answer perhaps is that adults want their children to perceive them as valued friends because they need companionship or do not want to be alone at the end of life. With this mind-set, life revolves around the children and the guilty feelings parents experience due to divorce. For instance, many children participate in different extracurricular activities daily regardless of the cost. Other examples include the many adults who are in financial debt due to holiday wishes, sweet sixteen parties, and automobile desires. An obvious consequence of this contemporary reality is that the more material possessions and opportunities parents provide, the less thankful many children appear and more disrespectful they seem. When adults act as friends rather than parents, they also often overprotect their youngsters. An example of this occurred when an eleven-year-old was asked how they were doing in school. The child standing alongside her mother stated, "I am getting As and Bs, but in Math, a C because the teacher assigns too much work and is crazy." What was shocking was that the mother stated that the lady was "crazy" in front of her child. So in other words, the C grade had everything to do with the teacher and not the student.

Another emotion -based family issue is the historical desire of parents to create a better life for their children than they had. With this mind-set, and the high standard of living many people experience, negative consequences sometimes result. For instance, some children appear to be missing out on opportunities to learn important life lessons because they are provided material possessions without working for them. An example was noticed when two tennis instructors were teaching tennis to a group of high school students. Many of the youth arrived in automobiles that were clearly nicer than the adults who both had multiple college degrees. One day, they looked at each other, and the younger instructor said, "That something is clearly wrong with this picture." Other examples can be found in any child's room or high school parking lot as students drive automobiles, have a gas card, and seem not to worry about insurance because someone else pays for those costs. Many children and adults today also seem to feel they are entitled to something simply because they were born. With this skewed perspective of reality, confusion naturally exists as to what individuals need and want. What once was perceived as desires are now something everyone should have— such as large homes, cell phones, and designer clothes. How can individuals be sensitive to others around them when they have a sense of entitlement or are confused between what they desire and truly need? This lack of sensitivity perhaps inadvertently taught in families provides one of many emotion-based barriers to broad societal change.

PLACES OF WORSHIP

Religion in its various forms is a major socializing agent in spite of being thought of by some as a divisive force in the world. Wars for example have been fought over the quest for religious freedom and various interpretations of the Bible or Koran have resulted in hatred and upheaval among different groups. Religion as well is presented in many instances as the answer to societal ills regardless of the issue of concern. It is not unusual to hear people state, "Everything has gone downhill since we have taken religion out of the schools," or "If people would be more godlike or focused on the Word everything would be better." An interesting aspect of these statements is how simplistic and condescending they seem. The interpretations of various religious stories also reflect how emotion results in adults relying on certain passages to answer important life questions. What is remarkable, however, is how angry some individuals become when you question their explanations or point out how it does not seem to connect with their daily behavior. Another characteristic of religion is how the written word appears to be presented abstractly, but most people think at a concrete level. Emotion is the logical reason as to why individuals accept intangible notions such as heaven and life ever after. Adults with limited abstract thinking abilities and lower literacy levels also seem to rely on literal interpretations of religious documents to guide their thoughts and actions. This self-serving, emotionally driven nature of religion contributes to why broad societal changes do not result; religion fuels the flame of emotion.

Religious institutions have also historically been local community gathering sites. For example, during slavery, it was reported that churches acted as fixtures for those who lacked freedom to congregate. Today, churches, temples, and mosques continue to meet the social needs of children and adults as large churches have become the norm in some areas of the United States. Religion at times also appears to be a smokescreen used to earn money as part of a large enterprising business. For instance, in some communities, churches compete with each other to have the largest building, the most services, and the highest-paid spiritual leader. An example of this ongoing quest for financial resources occurred during a recent church league basketball game. The minister of recreation who was officiating the game called a foul on a major financial contributor to the church. The church member proceeded to verbally argue that he did not harm anyone, and he was being discriminated against. After a lengthy emotionally heated discussion, the call was not reversed, and play continued with a general sense of uneasiness permeating the gym. Two days later, the recreation minister was asked to meet with the head pastor to discuss what had happened. She was strongly encouraged to meet with the church member and apologize; the implied message was, "We need his money, so work it out." Many other examples highlight how finances, rather than spiritual growth, are the focus of some religious organizations. How then can religious leaders be the moral compass for their local community if they are concerned about money rather than helping individuals reflect upon and perhaps change their daily behavior?

SCHOOLS

In a capitalistic society, the salaries of a profession normally reflect what is deemed important. Educators obviously are not highly valued because they are poorly compensated. Many adults simply believe that teaching is not difficult and anyone can do it. If that is the collective mindset, public education is in a quagmire due to those who work in schools. The age old statement "You get what you pay for" seems very appropriate in this case. If competitive salaries are not available, many talented individuals typically will not become educators. How then will the intellectual skills needed for personal emotional control and growth develop among youth if the majority of educators themselves do not possess those skills? Also, when state funding formulas contain an imbalance between sales and local property taxes, children who live in poor states with limited local property values are naturally discriminated against because the quality of their teachers may even be lower.

Another education issue is the curriculum content taught in schools. Recently, the discussion has revolved around preparing youth to enter the adult world with marketable employment skills. Is that merely what education is, preparing for future employment? What happened to the historical idea of exposing children to diverse content promoting intellectual curiosity, empowerment, and self-determination? In response to this corporate-driven mind-set, the federal government, despite limited constitutional authority, is influencing the curriculum experiences of the nation's youth. For instance, the United States Constitution indicates that issues not specifically stated within are the States's responsibility. Why, then, are states and local education agencies allowing the federal government to determine and often dictate education policies? Money is the obvious reason; the federal government influences the States through the allocation of tax dollars with the state demonstrating similar behavior to local municipalities. In other words, if the state does not comply with the federal government, they will lose tax dollars that are routinely not directly related to education (gas taxes used for roads and bridges), and the same is true for local communities in relationship to state mandates. Clearly, financial manipulation is impacting the educational experiences of America's youth. How then can broad societal changes occur if educators leading schools are not the most talented in society and the curriculum children experience is influenced by those who may have good intentions but limited knowledge of the local population?

Recent school shootings have also resulted in an emotion-based response. Many parents are now afraid that public schools are not safe and have decided to educate their children at home or in a private school to avoid youth who might possess a gun or have other challenging behavior. As this has happened, an interesting observation is the number of children present in grocery stores, malls, or restaurants and those who are wandering around their neighborhood unsupervised during typical school hours. The fearful emotions of adults are also naturally being transferred to children, possibly hindering or stymieing their academic growth and potential. How can a child learn if they are afraid of what might happen to them while at school? To offset and perhaps overcome these parental and student fears, state departments of education have adopted zero tolerance policies, required local school districts to design school safety plans, and requested reviews of codes of conduct. As a result, schools have become more structured and less accepting of difference. Children regardless of age are now required to sit at their desk quietly completing work as teachers follow a predetermined script with little flexibility in designing instructional lessons. Educational standardization may lessen parental fears; however, it has created an environment of control and order rather than personal empowerment.

MEDIA

The media is a major contributor to why broad societal changes do not occur. For many adults, when not working, time is spent passively observing television or searching for something of interest on the Internet. For many, daily life is basically getting up in the morning, going to work, coming home, and then watching television or playing on the computer the rest of the evening. This typical pattern of behavior may be the reason why some struggle with issues related to emotional intimacy and why many state they "are bored." Televisions and computers are entertainment tools that provide stimuli that ultimately kill or erase time. The real question though is, do individuals receive any joy from these actions or is it merely a filler activity that ultimately passes life away?

The information conveyed through the media is influencing how and what individuals think and believe. For example, twenty-four-hour television news stations allow individuals to be aware of events that they previously had no idea existed. At any moment, for instance, it is possible to obtain an update on the war in Afghanistan or view the damages caused by a cyclone in Bangladesh or the tornadoes in Australia. This increased access to information results in a variety of emotion -based responses ranging from personal validation and acceptance to a general sense of fear. In other words, adults can locate and identify with others who have similar experiences and are now aware of information that results in significant levels of discomfort. Another feature of the media is how it sometimes creates information. For instance, a number of years ago, a breaking story from Ohio was reported; a young person at an elementary school had fallen off the bleachers during a school assembly. The Cable News Network (CNN) provided footage of the ambulance arriving and followed the child to the local emergency room. The entire episode was perceived as comical because every day somewhere a child falls and gets hurt. The media also clearly impacts and shapes human emotions by the repeated coverage of major events and their negative aspects on life. How often do we have to view the planes crashing into the World Trade Center or the melting of the polar ice caps before we realize that the world is thought to be in peril?

An additional aspect of television and computers is how viewers seem to be in a constant quest for stimulating visual or auditory content. To capitalize on this, many television writers and computer website designers push the envelope as they develop story lines that peak curiosity and excitement. For example, in an hour-long television show, who would have thought that you would observe a person kissing multiple partners as they search for a life partner? Other television programs such as *Breaking Bad, Honey Boo Boo, South Park* and *Swamp People* are successful perhaps due to the shock value they provide viewers.

It too appears that in spite of having increasing numbers of television channels, many people can still not find content that does not contain some form of violence or sexuality. Sex and violence seems to be what individuals want to watch, and it also sells advertisements that create significant profits.

In summary, it is not possible to capture all the intricacies, nuances, and complexities of socialization. Rather, it is important to accept the fact that it has always been a part of the human condition and will continue throughout time. Socialization is a dynamic fluid process that provides a sense of order that societal members seek to feel safe and secure in life. As this aspect of the human experience evolves, families, places of worship, schools, and media will continue to influence the culture. With this thought in mind, it is important to identify and consider how socializing forces not only shape and impact a person's emotion and intellect but also lessen the likelihood of broad societal change.

SOCIALIZATION CONSEQUENCES: THE PROBLEM

A number of consequences arise from the socialization process. From a broad perspective, certain individuals or groups obtain higher status than others. Historically, skilled hunters and gatherers were valued due to the need to survive; now, individuals who are born into certain families (Kennedy and Bush), obtain monetary wealth (Trump, Stewart, and Winfrey), attend Ivy League schools, or entertain others receive elevated social standing. When members of society are perceived more important than others, a general sense of competition permeates the culture. This ingrained perspective is typically disseminated and often reinforced by the levels of education required for particular vocations. For instance, teachers are required to have four years of formal training before they can instruct children; a lawyer has six prior to practicing law, and medical doctors have at least eight before independently treating a patient. Another obvious delineation is found in the clothes various professions wear. Suits and ties are expected of lawyers, doctors have white coats, and educators wear casual attire. In other instances, if someone has their name stitched on their work clothes, members of society often perceive and treat them as though they are less capable than others. Another example of elevated social status is found with entertainers who have children with disabilities. Their physical appearance and role in a recent movie or television show allow them to have a forum to share their experiences when others do not. What message is sent when the media presents topics such as the dangers of plastic surgery (Kanye West) or the overdose of young hospitalized children (Dennis Quaid) only when it impacts a prominent individual and their family? Broad societal changes have limited chance of occurring when corporate leaders, athletes, musicians, and actors are perceived and treated differently than others.

A hierarchal social structure normally promotes the division of children and adults into categories based on some arbitrary criteria. The most noticeable example is the use of chronological age to determine appropriate behavior at a point of time in life. This common perspective is represented by the term "developmental milestones." For example, a toddler should begin to walk at one, and if they still are unable by the age of two, parents should be concerned. Professionals who use this perspective lead others to believe that the majority of children have been studied when they have not. In reality, can all sixteen-year-olds be the same? If not, why do each of them have the legal opportunity to drive an automobile in the United States? Are we also sure that some fourteen-year-olds are not capable of driving and other individuals regardless of their age should have access to motor vehicles?

Other legislation related to school attendance, employment, voting, marriage, social security, and political office reflect this frequent emotion-based socialization practice. Significant consequences seem to result when time is used to gain a sense of order; the most obvious is stereotyping based on age. Terms such as the *terrible twos*, *adolescence*, *middle age*, and *retirees* all invoke images of certain patterns of behavior that may not be true to all group members. Another related and perhaps pertinent observation is how the human experience seems to consist of a complete circle. Adults at the end of their life are treated similar to those at the beginning. Day care centers and convalescent homes seem to parallel each other as both attempt to provide food and shelter within a safe and stimulating environment. As members of society are conditioned to adopt this time-based perspective, their actions sometimes inadvertently oppress human potential while simultaneously promoting the undignified treatment of individuals and groups.

Children and adults who do not fit neatly in predetermined categories or boxes often scare people. In response to these uncomfortable feelings, other adults attempt to force them to conform. If they are incapable or unwilling to do so, they are often perceived as deficit in something, labeled, and then treated differently. This perspective is perpetuated by the medical fields of psychology and psychiatry through the use of the latest edition of the *Diagnostic Statistical Manual*. Yet, when you closely examine the criteria for each predetermined ailment, few physiological measures exist, and that what is listed is normal human behavior. What variables then differentiate a person from someone who has a conduct disorder (CD), obsessive-compulsive disorder (OCD), oppositional defiant disorder (ODD), or any other ailment? What is apparent is that the medical community can label anyone, anything, under the guise of helping. When this fact is pointed out to some medical professionals, they usually become defensive, stating that we need to label and categorize symptoms in order to provide treatment. Is that true or simply a statement that has been repeated over time that has become widely accepted? Another aspect of this common pattern of observing, labeling, and intervening is how standard protocols are developed for each medical condition. A recent example occurred when a friend had hip surgery. Rather than taking the time to discuss her needs, she was informed that certain pain medications were required to be taken, physical adaptations should occur within her home, and she needed counseling to overcome her recent difficulties. Needless to say, she became upset when someone without her knowledge attempted to modify her commode and scheduled a counseling session for her. Labeling human behavior and standardizing intervention protocols are examples of how emotion rather than intellect determines how people are perceived and treated by those around them. This common pattern of behavior may be one of the many reasons why broad societal changes have limited chance of occurring.

A lack of contentment is often a part of the socialization process. In response to this nagging sense of uneasiness, many adults search for something that they think is missing in their life that would make them feel complete or of greater value. Some, for example, struggle to determine if they would be happier with more money, an advanced educational degree, a large home in a given part of town, or some other material possession. As this ongoing "search and attempt to find" mentality develops, many adults ultimately adopt a personal perspective in which they determine their worth or value in comparison to others. Examples of this are evident each day. For instance, why do parents with limited resources purchase Nike shoes for their newborn; granted they look nice, but why spend large amounts of money on something that does not have anything to do with keeping their child's feet warm? The logical answer is that they want to be perceived favorably by those around them. Another related example is how some adults are willing to take huge financial risks to purchase a home that they really cannot afford. Many seem to be convinced that their life would be better if they had a place of their own. This norm-referenced life perspective clearly reflects how emotions impact personal decision making and human identity. If and when the vast majority of societal members adopt this point of view, it will naturally permeate governmental policies that impact the events of the world. For example, after September 11, 2001, security concerns resulted in many countries leveraging their assets to protect themselves and their interests. It is also evident when studying the multifaceted interconnecting issues related to oil prices, free trade agreements, and natural resources how world leaders are in a constant state of comparison and competition with each other. How can broad societal changes occur when the vast majority of individuals are in a constant state of "seeking and grasping in the air" for something they think will make things better?

Difficulties arise with a norm-referenced perspective on life. The most obvious is a general feeling that you have a lack of control in life. Many adults seem to believe that their experiences are "out of their hands" and their future will be determined by the people they know rather than their ability. With this mind-set, a sense of hopelessness, dependency, and a defeatist attitude is sometimes reflected in statements such as "Why should I try? It does not matter anyway," "What is the point of all of this?" or "I do not have any other choice." As these subconscious or conscious thoughts occur, individuals innately develop and establish daily routines that provide them a sense of safety and security rather than exploring options to possibly enhance their life. An example is sometimes noticed in an employment setting when a new corporate leader or employee is hired. A sense of uneasiness is usually present as that person may change something that has become the norm or raise the bar of expectations. In many cases, they will be viewed under the emotional "microscope" of others to determine if they will fit into the current way of thinking. In contrast, little time and energy is spent on determining what might be learned from the new leader or employee. Another emotion-based illustration is noticed when college graduates obtain their first teaching position. Feelings of anxiety and vulnerability often cause them to gravitate toward someone who is physically similar to their mother, father, or close friend in order to feel more secure. In other instances, their need for acceptance results in behavior that they would not normally demonstrate.

Adults also tend to exaggerate when they determine their value in comparison to others. In many instances, what is experienced and shared with family and friends is not an accurate account of what really happened. A comical historical example is the fisherman who tells the story of the fish that got away. Often the fish is reported to have been larger than the boat and that it would have taken hours to reel in. Similar to anglers, those who have a need for acceptance often distort their view of themselves while participating in the activities of daily living. For instance, how can a tennis player become angry with the way in which they are playing if they have not participated in any physical activity for eight weeks? Why would you throw the racket against the fence several times and state, "It is time to give up this game," if you had an accurate assessment of your athletic ability? Many other embellishments seem to occur when someone describes the abilities of their child, the importance of their job, how wonderful a vacation was, and the intensity of sorrow they felt with the loss of a loved one. As these distorted outward expressions of emotion are occurring, their intensity sometimes paralyzes individuals. This common, but not typically thought about everyday reality often results in adults making negative lifestyle choices, such as inappropriately spending money, not exercising or eating well, and relying on substances to gain some form of relief. The emotions conveyed through the statement, "I am so stressed, and I am just having such a hard time with everything," perhaps also indicates how little adults know about the power of their emotions. This lack of understanding coupled with ongoing emotional stress increases the risk for a heart attack, stroke, or other medical maladies.

VICTIMIZATION: A SOCIETAL REALITY

The emotions associated with socialization-related problems often result in a sense of victimization. Victimization can be defined as physical or emotional harm ranging from overt (physical) to covert actions (lack of emotional support or opportunities) that stymie human potential. What is deemed as victimization is typically reflected in the values of society at a particular point in time. For example, since the 1960s, many programs have been established to help those who have limited food, shelter, and educational opportunities. What is interesting though is when you talk with adults who lived during the Depression era (1930s); they share what it was like being poor but do not mention poverty. To them, they had a roof over their head and enough food to eat and no one was better off than anyone else. Another more recent issue is the concern associated with children and adults who are impulsive; impulsivity has been linked to problems ranging from credit card debt to domestic violence. These and other perceived problems have led to research ideas and specific disciplines. Granted, some scientific discoveries have resulted in increased life spans and technological advancements; others, however, have relied on and perhaps taken advantage of the emotions of others for self-gain. Examples are studies of birth order. Some researchers have concluded that firstborn children are leaders, middle is negotiators and problem solvers, and the youngest is creative but the most undisciplined. As simplistic as this appears, even more bizarre is how scholars present pictures of historical and contemporary figures to support their theory. It too is clear that when many adults cannot understand something, philosophical or theoretical constructs, such as neuroeconomics, neuromapping, and phantom ring syndrome are developed in order to gain some sense of order.

As individuals gain experiences in life, they seem to adopt a belief that they have been harmed in someway by a particular aspect of society. A common feature of this emotion-based reality is that some appear stuck, unable to change their life, as their identity becomes whatever is their problem. An example is sometimes noticed with those who struggle with depression; everything seems to revolve around how they are feeling rather than the specific experiences they are having at the moment. This sense of discomfort, pain, and self- doubt usually results in two distinct patterns of behavior. Adults to some degree either emotionally withdraw from others or openly discuss their difficulties to gain attention and support. In most cases, those who withdraw insulate themselves by placing an emotional barrier similar to an imaginary fence around them. Individuals, for example, who recently experienced divorce often state, "I will not allow myself to be vulnerable, and I will never marry again." This "doom and gloom" mentality often results in them projecting their pain on others. An example of this occurred while talking to a student who had just completed a college course. It was obvious to the professor that she was bright; yet, she did not perform well in class. After discussing her course grade, she disclosed how elementary school teachers used to tell her that she was "stupid and would not amount to anything." Thirty years later, she still struggles with test anxiety. On the opposite end of the emotional spectrum are adults who volunteer their difficulties with anyone who will listen. As they disclose information, it is almost as though they are looking for a certain reaction in order to validate their problems or sense of victimization. What has become increasingly clear though is that individuals who demonstrate this verbal purging are seeking attention, do not have the skills necessary to change their plight in life, or are simply lazy and would rather discuss their problems rather than adapting their behavior.

Another observation regarding problems and victimization is how individuals become emotionally comfortable with certain aspects of life while simultaneously searching for something to feel better in other areas. This is evident, when browsing the aisles of any bookstore, as thousands if not millions of self-help books, such as *The Purpose Driven Life*, *Seven Habits of Highly Effective People*, *The Power of Positive Thinking* , and *Atkins Diet*, are purchased each day. As adults search for answers to important life questions, emotion -based thoughts often surface. For example, many believe that to improve your plight in life, you simply have to pull yourself up by the "bootstraps" by working harder and obtaining an education. If that is true, all individuals must have the same genetic endowment and experiences. Another widely accepted belief is that if a person has a certain attitude or performs good deeds, such as contributing to the United Way and Salvation Army; the Ultimate Being will protect them and improve their life. This line of thinking perhaps is why some academics spend an inordinate amount of time writing grants promoting innovative ideas. What is astounding is how even if the grant is not funded, their efforts seem to cause them to feel better. These emotion-based thoughts captured in a sense of false hope divert attention from the reality that all individuals to some degree feel they have been victims of something.

COMMON RESPONSES TO VICTIMIZATION

There are many responses to a sense of victimization. The most common appears to be a reliance on tradition to gain a sense of order and safety. An example sometimes occurs when a person is in an intensive care unit. Family members are conditioned to believe that they should spend their entire day at the hospital and visit their loved one each time an opportunity exists. In actuality, the entire process may hinder recovery and promote constant emotional upheaval for those involved. Another traditional belief is reflected in the structure of many public institutions. In education, for instance, many think that someone first must be a teacher, assistant principal, or principal and work in the central office prior to becoming a school superintendent. It is believed that individuals have to experience various types of positions along the career ladder before ultimately obtaining a leadership position. In other words, the field of public education, and perhaps the majority of society, is comprised of professionals spending years of their working life underemployed until some arbitrary standard is met for them to obtain a professional opportunity they are already qualified to perform.

A number of other coping strategies are used to offset the discomfort and pain associated with a sense of victimization. The most obvious is an individual's perspective on life. For many, a quantitative rather than qualitative viewpoint provides a simple, tangible means to determine worth or value. An example is the emphasis placed on obtaining money to purchase goods, services, and opportunities. What is interesting though is how the struggle for wealth results in a set of its own emotionally charged problems, such as inequality, cheating, gambling, and embezzlement. In other instances, adults distract their attention from ongoing emotional discomfort by creating statements such as "This too will pass" or "It is what it is." Other attempts may sometimes include participating in athletics, attending religious institutions, praying, and using substances such as alcohol and other drugs. Despite these common patterns of behavior, emotion creates a general atmosphere of victimization and an ongoing sense of mistrust. This causes many to become defensive, judgmental, opinionated, and unwilling to accept those who are significantly different from themselves. As this naturally unfolds, broad societal changes have limited chance of occurring.

In the end, a sense of victimization causes many individuals to believe their life experiences will be determined by someone other than themselves. Adults with this mind-set usually rely on the government to meet their most basic needs. A natural outcome of this emotion-based perspective is the need for external oversight. In most disciplines serving the public, professionals now spend hours each day completing paperwork that documents compliance with existing policies and procedures.

As one medical professional recently stated, "How can I provide therapy if I have to complete all this paperwork for Joint Commission's visit?" Another example is when a newly appointed college administrator stated "that his goals were to make sure that the university does not lose any of its accreditation under his watch." Individuals and institutions seem afraid of governing bodies as they often are perceived as the boogie man, invisible in the corner of the room trying to catch you doing something wrong. What might be considered both amusing and sad is how specific education levels are required for certain jobs; however, once individuals obtain the desired qualifications, they need to be monitored. Many legal concerns also arise with this general feeling of victimization. For example, it is not uncommon to hear, "Legally we have to do this, or we cannot do that because it may not be on high legal grounds." What does that mean, and how much documentation is needed to demonstrate that you have not violated anyone's rights? Other policies and procedures associated with identity theft (social security numbers), banking (photo IDs), and electronic transmission of information (security codes) illustrate how a small percentage of citizens can create a sense of fear among people. It is painfully obvious that broad societal changes have limited chance of occurring when the vast majority of societal members have an unrelenting sense of victimization.

CHAPTER SUMMARY

Broad societal changes do not occur because it is impossible to significantly alter the emotional and intellectual traits of human beings. This historical and ongoing reality of life is the reason why individuals continue to harm others, certain groups cannot live in harmony resulting in wars, and someone has to die before a traffic light is placed at a busy intersection. It too is clear that the energy generated from emotion more so than intellect is the variable that ultimately determines the likelihood of change. This aspect of the human experience was evident when reviewing some of the contemporary issues associated with the family, places of worship, school, and information gained from the media. Another key discovery in this process was that most life stories—regardless of gender, culture, economic situation, educational level, or any other significant indicator—contain a series of problems and general sense of victimization.

Victimization was defined as physical or emotional harm ranging from overt (physical) to covert actions (lack of emotional support or opportunities) that hinder the identification and nurturance of human potential. This acute and chronic sense of discomfort and pain causes many individuals to believe that their life experiences will be determined by someone other than themselves. Those with this mind-set generally rely on traditional beliefs and the government to guide their actions. More specifically, however, adults to some degree emotionally respond to victimization by withdrawing from others or openly discussing their difficulties to gain needed support. In spite of these typical patterns of behavior, the emotions associated with victimization create an ongoing sense of mistrust. This causes many to become defensive, judgmental, opinionated, and unwilling to accept those who are significantly different from themselves. As this naturally unfolds in the activities of daily living, broad societal changes have limited chance of occurring.

In the upcoming chapter, the human indoctrination process will be explored to illuminate the role of emotion in life. An increased understanding of this natural aspect of the human experience may increase the likelihood that individuals will spend their energy living in the moment rather than thinking about the past or what might happen in the future.

INDOCTRINATION: EMOTIONS IMPACT ON LIFE

Broad societal changes do not occur because the emotional and intellectual traits of human beings cannot be significantly altered. This is clear when you consider how life's journey begins within an existing culture containing mores and values that provide the sense of order needed to feel safe and secure. Families, places of worship schools, and media, then, to some degree shape the developing child's thoughts and actions. For most, the innate need for love and belonging coupled with limited intellectual ability, results in the acceptance of information without question. This feature of the human experience is sometimes reflected in beliefs such as "If you work hard, you will have a good life." That may be true for some; however, for others, a causal relationship between effort and outcome has little impact on determining quality of life. A number of other interrelated, multifaceted outcomes result from this typical indoctrination process. The most obvious is that creative thought may not be valued. Children and adults who have ideas that create discomfort for others often are judged, avoided, and isolated. In extreme cases, various labels are assigned (ADHD, OCD, and ODD), and corresponding interventions are implemented. As this occurs, cultural structures naturally develop and evolve with certain individuals perceived as valuable while others are devalued. Many other similar observations provide proof of the strength of emotion in the human indoctrination process. Some of which will be discussed in the upcoming chapter.

INDOCTRINATION

Indoctrination is the process of instilling ideas and attitudes (Snook, 1972). Arthur (2003) suggested that to indoctrinate is to teach something that is universally accepted regardless of evidence to the contrary or in the absence of any proof. If indoctrination is the promotion of a single unassailable view, education is the opposite. Education promotes the exploration of alternative viewpoints, the critical application of data and argument, and the development of skills and dispositions necessary to act on the information. Assuming that this differentiation between indoctrination and education is accurate, why do people appear to rely on traditional beliefs rather than science to guide their thoughts and actions? The answer to this important question is human emotion. Emotion consists of complex layers of processes that are in constant contact with the environment. At a minimum, these interactions include cognitive stimuli appraisal, or evaluation of meaning, and physical changes such as endocrine, autonomic, and cardiovascular. Emotion is the energy that drives, organizes, amplifies, and attenuates cognitive activity within the socially influenced, value-appraising process of the brain (Siegel, 1999). These internal feelings range from primitive reflexes and responses (instincts) to multifaceted complexities described and labeled as happiness, anger, joy, sadness, guilt, fear, hope, and love.

To further explore the link between emotion and indoctrination, an understanding of information processing theory might be helpful. Three assumptions guide this approach (Searleman and Herrmann, 1994). Information is obtained in distinct stages beginning with attending to a stimulus, followed by recognition, transformation into mental representation, comparisons with data existing in memory, assigning meaning, and acting in some fashion. Second, there are limits on how much information can be processed at each stage. Although the absolute amount that can be learned is limitless, it must be acquired gradually. Third, the human information-processing system is interactive. Children and adults respond to environmental stimuli based on past events; that which is experienced affects and determines what is known (Searleman and Herrmann, 1994). The processing of information begins with the sensory register, the first memory store (Snowman, McCown, and Biehler, 2009). Its purpose is to hold for one to three seconds an unending series of sounds and images. If stimuli is recognized and then thought about, it will be processed and transferred to short -term memory. Short term-memory holds approximately seven unrelated bits of data for twenty seconds and is referred to as working memory (Hambrick and Engle, 2003). Data is then transferred to long- term memory if maintenance and elaborative rehearsal activities occur. Long-term memory is an unlimited permanent record of everything an individual has learned (Schunk, 2004). This store of information is organized and summarized in abstract schemata. When these structures are well formed and a specific event is consistent with expectations, comprehension occurs. If poorly constructed or absent, learning is slow and uncertain (Moreno, 2006).

Emotion naturally plays a role in information processing. When encountering and reacting to environmental stimuli, emotion, more so than intellect, seems to determine certain responses and what is ultimately stored in long -term memory.

For example, an individual's current psychological state influences the type and amount of information acquired and retained. It appears that if someone has had a series of negative experiences, such as a job loss, illness, or financial difficulty, they are more likely to expend energy emitting basic survival instincts rather than obtaining information. To think more about this feature of the human condition, a cardinal scale beginning with one (no negative sensations) ending with ten (extreme discomfort) could be developed. Points along the continuum represent the amount of distress present. The higher the level, the more likely someone would fail to notice opportunities to gain information. In extreme trauma, adults may lose days, months, or even years of possibilities. Emotion clearly plays a significant role in interpreting and determining what information is heard, observed, and stored in memory. Now that we have briefly explored emotion and information processing theory, it is time to return to indoctrination.

A number of variables are associated with indoctrination. The most obvious is the innate human characteristics that allow individuals to be indoctrinated. Locke's (1690) concept of tabula rasa provides a rationale as he suggests that infants are born without thoughts, and knowledge is obtained through experiences derived from the senses. He also stated that the "association of ideas" made when young are more important than those acquired later in life. If one accepts Locke's premises, primitive instincts would act to filter information from the environment. Evidence of this may be reflected in some of the basic principles of survival of the fittest. Those with greater physical and intellectual prowess naturally influence the behavior of those around them. It too appears that as individuals have become more sophisticated in their use of language, certain institutions perpetuate this ongoing imbalance of power. Formal education is one such example.

Many are conditioned to believe that a particular academic degree reflects the ability to perform a certain task or function. This way of thinking typically results in the creation of hierarchical structures that inadvertently promote a sense of insecurity, helplessness, and dependence on others.

Human relationships provide the foundation for the indoctrination process. The characteristics of these interactions are often based on a doctrine containing a charismatic leader. An example is the various Christian typologies and their respective beliefs. McLaren (2004) described some of them as the following:

1. Those who are considered Conservative Protestants think that people are guilty of sin and wrongdoing. The good news is that Jesus's death pays the full penalty for human sin.
2. Pentecostal followers believe that the human race is suppressed by disease and poverty. Jesus teaches us how to receive miracles and healings from God through faith in his promises.
3. Roman Catholics think that people are enslaved by the fear of death and Jesus's resurrection defeats demise, liberating humanity.
4. Eastern Orthodox followers describe how human beings are spiritually sick and need healing as they have dropped out of the dance of creation. To overcome this problem, Jesus's incarnation into humanity and history brings God's healing to the human race and all creation.
5. Liberal Protestants state that people suffer from ignorance of the teaching and way of Christ and that Jesus's example and teachings should inspire us to work compassionately for social justice.
6. Anabaptists focus on how individuals are divided, violent, and in need to learn the ways of Christ in order to promote love and peace.
7. Liberation theology believers focus on how humanity is oppressed by corrupt powers and systems and how Jesus commissions and leads bands of activities to confront unjust

regimes (McLaren, 2004).

In spite of these various religious delineations, there are many crossovers and hybrids among visions of Jesus. An example is how most Pentecostals share a close affinity with Conservative Protestants in their attention to human guilt and the forgiveness Jesus's death brings. Many Catholics as well share a concern for social justice with Liberal Protestants and Anabaptists and Liberationists. Each of these groups also have nuances, substreams, counterstreams, weaknesses, problems, and minority opinions as evidenced by the varying interpretations of content within the same denomination (McLaren, 2004). Regardless of the many differences in general viewpoint between and within generations of each religious sect, the statement, "Do onto others as you would have done on to you" seems to provide the foundation for human interaction.

Religious doctrines also provide the moral underpinning for the rule of law. Laws not only represent shared beliefs, they too are a major component of the indoctrination process. Information related to what is legally acceptable behavior is typically disseminated from one generation to the next by family, places of worship, schools, and media. Laws as well reflect the multifaceted and evolving nature of human values. One such example is associated with the multiple interpretations of an action. For instance, various countries around the world participate in military conflicts because harming someone in the name of protecting your country is heroic; however, if you exhibited the same behavior in your local community, you might be placed in a mental institution or correctional facility. Another case in point is associated with the reason why certain substances such as alcohol and cigarettes are legal when marijuana and cocaine are not. How can these differences be explained? The answer may be associated with how human emotion is reflected in the intent, reading, and enforcement of a particular law. Other statements such as "Even though something might be legal, it does not mean it is right" provides further evidence of how religious beliefs impact the rule of law.

Now that the general parameters for behavior have been established, the process of indoctrination begins with shared physical space and a channel of communication. Initially, an idea, perception, or feeling is conveyed nonverbally and in spoken or written language. The listener then interprets the message based on their personal reality. Once meaning has been assigned, a corresponding nonverbal and verbal response is emitted. This ongoing sequence of events typically continues until a participant voluntarily stops talking, walks away, or does not respond to an electronic transmission of information. Successful communication is normally thought to have occurred if the perceived message approximates the intent of the sender. As individuals communicate, emotion and intellect are naturally interconnected. Nevertheless, personal observations and corresponding reflections illuminate how emotion more so than intellect acts as the major source of energy needed to indoctrinate someone.

Operant conditioning also plays a significant role in indoctrination. Skinner (1983) suggested that voluntary responses are strengthened when followed by a desirable consequence and weakened when ignored or punished. As infants begin to use their senses to explore their environment, they instinctively adopt behaviors of those around them. This is sometimes noticed when a child walks similar to one of their parents. As children become older, positive reinforcement coupled with the avoidance of punishment guides the development of most thoughts. As this indoctrination process continues, emotion often shapes and determines what individuals ultimately believe. For example, the abstract meanings assigned to words such as *happiness*, *joy*, and *love* are frequently used to evaluate one's life. These reference points are sometimes reflected in questions such as "Are you happy? Do you obtain joy from your work? Have you found someone to love?" When negative feelings arise to these and other similar questions, adults seem conditioned to think that they are missing out on an important aspect of life or have become a victim of something. Similar thoughts also appear to surface when adults do not have children, live in poverty, or have been provided few opportunities by their parents. Despite what many are indoctrinated to believe, life experiences may be neither good nor bad, but rather simply expenditures of energy.

A simple balloon analogy may further illustrate the role of emotion in indoctrination. The balloon represents an idealized mental image of a family, job, home, life experience, or other valued facet of life. As daily activities occur, how individuals respond to the inflation (moving closer to the image) or deflation (moving away from the image) of their balloons determine if they will nurture or oppress their innate abilities. For instance, how a father reacts in response to his desired image of coaching his son may impact how he perceives himself and his child. It seems relatively clear in this situation that if adults have an internal sense of calmness, they increase the likelihood of reaching the contents within their balloons. In contrast, those who respond emotionally and instinctively place some value (good, bad, wonderful, disappointing) on their experiences lessen the chance of reaching their desired outcomes. When thinking more about the inflation and deflation of balloons, Kubler-Ross's (1969) stages of death and dying provides a logical explanation of how individuals typically respond. Initially, adults deny that their balloon is incongruent with reality and impossible to achieve. As time passes, they become angry when realizing that regardless of their efforts, they will not experience what is included within their balloon. For some, they will bargain with a higher power to gain the necessary support needed. When denial, anger, and bargaining fail, the individual becomes depressed prior to accepting that a certain aspect of life represented within the balloon will not happen. Once reaching this point, they have the opportunity to recalibrate their balloon while simultaneously nurturing their talent. In an ideal world, however, emotion's role in the indoctrination process would be one that did not influence the balloons associated with hopes, dreams, and desires. Rather, individuals would identify and experience the feeling, manage the energy associated with it, and then begin anew. Each response would not be dominated by an emotion-laden perspective but rather a more objective viewpoint. For this to happen, adults would need to explore how their perception of reality has been shaped and reinforced by the evolving, multifaceted indoctrination process. If enough people adopt this self-awareness perspective, energy might become available to increase the likelihood of individual and collective change.

LIFE: LIVING IN A TUNNEL

The indoctrination process can be described using a tunnel example. The width of the tunnel represents the mores and values of society, and the length is average life expectancy. When individuals enter (birth) the tunnel, parents and siblings begin to bombard them with information, shaping their present and future way of thinking. As they continue to muddle and plod along within, their emotional needs cause them to often remain without question. If they do, however, temporarily or permanently leave, others such as spouses, family, and friends attempt to pull them back using traditional beliefs, laws, and physical force. For those who do escape, they are often thought of as deficit in something, labeled, and in need of support. Once they gain needed assistance, it is generally believed that they will realize the error in their ways and reenter the tunnel. For those who still resist, they will often be perceived as dangerous, in need of constant supervision and oversight. What is also evident is that the dimensions of the tunnel act paradoxically. The width and length provide the sense of order needed for some to identify and nurture their talent while for others it acts to oppress innate ability. It too seems relatively clear that in order for skills to be identified and nurtured, the dimensions of the tunnel have to become wider, veering in various directions.

Maslow's (1968) ideas can be used to organize and describe how emotion presents itself within the tunnel. He suggested that physiological needs are the most primitive, followed in ascending order by safety, belonging and love, esteem, and self-actualization. The lower the need is, the greater its strength. For example, in the case of extreme hunger, children and adults will stop trying to satisfy a higher-level need such as safety or esteem until their basic life-sustaining requirements are met. Maslow also indicated that physiological, safety, belongingness, and love are deficiency needs because they motivate individuals to act only when they are unmet to some degree. Self-actualization, by contrast, is considered a growth need as individuals strive to satisfy it by developing their potential talents and capabilities. Despite the obvious oversimplification and linear description of human needs, Maslow's ideas will be used to represent the various chambers of the tunnel.

PHYSIOLOGICAL CHAMBER

The most important chamber within the tunnel is physiological.

Human beings require a certain amount of food and water in order to exist. If unmet, muscles begin to atrophy, the immune system becomes compromised, and ultimately, major organs no longer function. In response to these basic necessities of life, a number of indoctrinated beliefs have been created and perpetuated throughout time. The most obvious is that three meals a day are needed in order to obtain and maintain optimal health. If individuals eat breakfast, lunch, and dinner, they are led to believe that they will gain essential nutrients. Adults are even conditioned to think that certain foods should be eaten only at particular meals. For example, cereal is for breakfast rather than lunch or dinner, and pizza is not appropriate to eat at the beginning of day. The concept of "feeling full" is another emotion-based example. Many children and adults are conditioned to eat until they feel a certain physiological response. This sensation appears to be associated in some way with a positive feeling as reflected in the statement, "You should be happy because at least you have enough food to eat."

Emotional intimacy is also often intertwined with basic physiological needs. In many instances, food is the common variable in which individuals gather to celebrate a certain accomplishment or event. Youth are also taught that they should offer guests a beverage or meal, and if they do not partake when offered, they may offend their host. Other examples of this are present in the dating process. For some, an ideal date is dining at a restaurant or having a picnic in an idyllic setting. Food appears to not only fulfill basic physiological needs, it also provides a sense of comfort. In other situations, acute or chronic emotional difficulties may lead to an imbalance between the amount consumed and that which is needed. Another issue associated with intimacy is the primitive need for sex. For most individuals, physical attraction acts as the beginning of a possible relationship. As time passes, a feeling of closeness may lead to sexual activities. Having sex is not simply associated with procreation; it also results in a physiologically based response that is sometimes labeled and described as love. In many adult relationships, sex is thought to equal love, and without sex, emotional intimacy does not exist.

A number of other emotion-based behaviors surface in the physiological chamber of the tunnel. It seems that when basic needs are met, individuals are more likely to develop a positive self-image and an opportunistic outlook toward life. This demeanor results in a sense of empowerment, a willingness to work with others, and a general belief that regardless of what is experienced, everything will be all right. In contrast, those who do not have their most basic needs met appear to create and live in an atmosphere of fear and anxiety. It is also evident that as the intensity of discomfort increases, emotion more so than intellect determines and guides behavior. An example was witnessed in the aftermath of Hurricane Katrina. Many of those affected appeared scared that they might not have enough food to eat or receive appropriate medical attention. What was obvious to most onlookers though was that several of them exceeded the World Health Organization weight recommendations and experienced only minor injuries. Regardless of the particular circumstances, children and adults instinctively become more self-centered when their basic needs are not met. Evidence of this is present almost everywhere, as most human actions to some degree are self-serving rather than altruistic.

Adults who struggle to meet their basic needs are often conditioned to believe that there must be something inherently wrong with them. This self-doubt is reflected in questions such as "Why is my life this way?" or "Why can I not obtain a job to pay my bills?" This feeling of helplessness sometimes manifests into anger and a tendency to blame others for difficulties. In most cases, parents receive the brunt of criticism; "If only my mother would have nurtured me more or if we would not have moved so often, I would not be in this terrible predicament." These negative self-thoughts seem to result in a sense of urgency to alleviate discomfort and pain. This aspect of the human experience may be one reason why the medical community has grown and financially thrived in the name of helping. The emotions associated with the thought of death might explain too why patients willingly wait for hours to see a doctor or participate in various invasive procedures. Another medical issue is the need to have insurance. Without it, people are led to believe they will not receive appropriate care, will suffer needlessly, or die when their life could have been prolonged.

A number of other indoctrinated beliefs surround those who struggle in the physiological chamber of the tunnel. From a broad perspective, many are conditioned to believe that they should help those in need. By doing so, they are demonstrating acts of caring perceived favorably by a higher power. One such example is the many television commercials containing images of insects landing on the faces of malnourished infants and commentators simultaneously stating, "For only a dollar a day, you can help this child receive the food he needs." These emotional appeals garner significant amounts of money despite evidence indicating that only a small percentage of donations reach those in need. An alternative viewpoint is also present. A number of adults believe that those who struggle should be held accountable for their negative actions and work harder in order to improve their plight in life. This line of thinking is reflected in the idea of social mobility and the obtainment of the American Dream. Regardless of the perspective held, a variety of questions arise. For example, do individuals who give money to charitable organizations gain more from the donation than those who receive it? Does episodic or ongoing support help the downtrodden, or is it cruel to provide false hope to those who have limited chance of self-subsistence? Also, if effort is the main variable determining quality of life, what role do genetic differences play in life experiences? Responses to these questions and others illuminate how physiological needs act as the tunnel's foundation.

SAFETY CHAMBER

A sense of personal safety is needed to experience the many aspects of the tunnel. Without it, individuals primarily rely on basic instincts to function in the activities of daily living. Throughout history, however, a number of indoctrinated responses have surfaced and evolved to move beyond primitive actions. The most obvious is the development and use of language to label and describe phenomenon. A common example of this occurs when someone visits a doctor to gain a diagnosis and explanation for their current condition. The information usually lessens anxiety and helps determine what can be done to feel better. It also appears that once something has been defined, adults can avoid feeling afraid and isolated by talking about it with others. In other instances, if acute or persistent periods of insecurity exist, individuals are taught to refrain from participating in certain activities such as air travel. Another common way of thinking to promote personal safety is comparing your plight in life to someone else. Many seem to feel better regarding the realities of their own experiences after observing the graphic images of violence in Libya or starvation in Rwanda. This pattern of behavior acts as a defense mechanism to distort and possibly escape uncomfortable feelings.

Other emotional buffers and distracters are present in the safety chamber of the tunnel. Without them, some adults would experience such a high level of discomfort that they may not be able to function in the activities of daily living. Logically, parents, guardians, and friends are the most common buffers relied upon when problems arise. Distractions, on the other hand, are conditioned responses and activities that allow individuals to temporarily escape difficult feelings. These diversions present themselves in a variety of ways. For example, children and adults are taught that they should establish personal goals. They too are conditioned to believe that optimal health is associated with finding a balance between work and participation in leisure activities. What may be lost in this line of thinking is that the self-imposed pressure to reach goals might be more detrimental than beneficial and someone could experience a high level of joy from their vocation. Another common belief is that life is difficult, often miserable at times, and adults should try to temporarily escape from it. This idea might explain why television has become a staple in the lives of many and why entertainers seem to receive higher status and levels of compensation than law enforcement officers and teachers.

Despite the emotional support gained through buffers and distracters, many in the tunnel still struggle with personal safety. This ongoing sense of uneasiness causes them to believe that various laws are needed to promote social order. Without them, violence and chaos would result. This perspective may be true in some situations; however, unintended outcomes seem to result. The most notable is the message sent to children that rules are needed because people are unable to function without them. Adults also lose a certain level of personal freedom when they voluntarily allow others to shape and guide their actions. For example, the majority of individuals in the United States believe the government is capable of understanding and solving local community problems. This traditional belief coupled with instinctive responses seems to provide the level of emotional comfort and stability needed to function within the tunnel. It too may possibly explain why most adults appear comfortable with sameness and uneasy with the thought of change.

When further considering the safety chamber of the tunnel, it would be remiss not to mention Freud's (1938) ideas. He suggested that individuals respond to environmental stimuli in ways that provide comfort and emotional balance. When certain experiences though consistently trigger physiological -based responses, they are often labeled and considered negative rather than positive. Therefore, the quality of life is determined by the intensity and accumulation of discomfort and pain. Freud's ideas still appear relevant today. For instance, to some degree, individuals are fearful of those who are different from them. This sense of uneasiness may be the reason why many have difficulty interacting with others who do not share the same gender, race, socioeconomic level, or way of thinking. Additional evidence of this is apparent when considering the number of adults who have friends similar to them, adopt lifestyles like their parents, and read books by authors that support their existing point of view. These common patterns of behavior act as forms of emotional self-insulation that increase the likelihood of obtaining feelings of belonging and love.

BELONGING AND LOVE CHAMBER

As newborns enter the tunnel, they join approximately seven billion others. Despite this large population, limited interactions occur with those much different from them. Why is this? A possible reason is that human beings instinctively form groups and adopt collective points of view in order to insulate themselves from individuals who look, think, and act dissimilar. Another possible answer is that without a general sense of personal safety, it is difficult and perhaps impossible to experience certain levels of belonging and love. However, if it is obtained, these feelings may be described as physiological-based responses that result in positive energy. An example sometimes occurs when individuals gain comfort from each other by stating, "I love you."

From a broad perspective, the ongoing quest for belonging and love may be the reason why human beings are vulnerable to indoctrination. All individuals to some degree want to feel a part of something and that someone cares about them. These feelings begin to develop when infants and care providers interact. In most instances, if adequate amounts of physical and emotional support are present, the child will have an increased chance of obtaining positive energy. Conversely, if what is needed is not present, they may have limited periods in life when they feel belonging and love. Children also seem innately programmed to believe that positive feelings or energy is somehow associated with acting like those in their environment. This typical thought process seems to result in the development and reliance on various theories to explain certain actions. Smith's (1991) capitalism ideas may be one such example. He suggested that specialization leads to the creation of quality goods and services that promote economic benefit. Within each discipline and subspecialty, individuals share an identity in which certain terminology is used to promote group cohesion. This form of professional self-segregation leads to a platform in which adults may gain a sense of belonging and perhaps even love.

The search for belonging and love continues as individuals muddle and plod along in the tunnel. In most cases, children and adults gravitate toward others who are physically similar to them; if obvious commonalities are not present, they walk in the direction of those who have characteristics like family and friends who have provided them a sense of safety in the past. Once in shared space, communication patterns then act as the means for initiating, continuing, and possibly developing relationships that provide a feeling of belonging and love. What is evident in this process is how adults are conditioned to believe certain emotion-based statements or questions. Two common examples are "What does your gut tell you about him?" or "How do you feel about it?" This tendency to rely more so on emotion rather than intellect reflects how human instincts manifest and present themselves in some shape and form in most if not all actions.

Common interests also appear to shape the experiences in the belonging and love chamber of the tunnel. When an individual talks with someone about a mutually valued topic, they increase the likelihood of obtaining a sense of belonging and love. This is evident when observing and listening to two individuals interested in antique automobiles. Their initial conversations focus solely on the topic until they reach a certain level of comfort. Once obtained, future discussions unrelated to antique automobiles normally occur. What sometimes also happens is that when individuals begin to trust each other, they introduce their new acquaintance to other friends who have similar interests. In spite of this simplistic linear account of events, moving from acquaintance relationships to friendships is the cornerstone of the belonging and love chamber of the tunnel. As one might then expect, emotions experienced during past relationships surface and shape what is currently felt. Those who have had many negative encounters seem more likely to have limited numbers of friends compared to those who have had positive relationships. This reality of life may be the reason why some adults think that friendships are difficult. It too may explain why adults are conditioned to believe that if they have had five good friends at the end of their life, they have had a good life.

A number of other thoughts come to mind when thinking about the belonging and love chamber of the tunnel. One is that individuals create their own reality. This fluid aspect of the human condition results in certain actions perceived as love by some and not others. For many, high levels of ambiguity and uneasiness will cause them to leave the belonging and love chamber. As they exit, their level of emotional vulnerability seems to determine if they will gain comfort from catchphrases or slogans such as "It is what it is" and "This too will pass." Another observation is how people naturally self-segregate. It appears that within each ongoing subsystem, categories develop and evolve based on the innate characteristics of those present. As this unfolds, hierarchical structures seem to form in which certain individuals are perceived as more valuable than others. What is also evident is how many adults are conditioned to believe that they should strive to climb the hierarchy. To do so, many adapt and even comprise their principles in order to rationalize behaviors they normally would not exhibit. Another aspect of this typical chain of events is how subgroups commonly seek members in order to influence and compete against each other. For example, liberals, conservatives, and moderates are thought to significantly vary in their line of thinking; yet, they appear to have more commonalities than differences. Lastly, it would be remiss not to mention how individuals having alternative viewpoints struggle in the belonging and love chamber of the tunnel. They often create such a level of discomfort for others that they are isolated and sometimes targets of harsh treatment. In extreme cases, they are perceived as members of fringe groups that represent misguided notions that are in constant need of monitoring.

ESTEEM CHAMBER

Adults entering the esteem chamber of the tunnel desire strength, achievement, autonomy, competence, confidence, independence, and freedom (Maslow, 1968). They also yearn for respect, status, fame, and glory. Satisfaction of these needs help individuals feel self-confident, worthy, capable, adequate, and useful in the world (Maslow, 1968). Without them, feelings of inferiority, weakness, and helplessness may permeate the activities of daily living. Maslow's esteem ideas reflect how emotion impacts identity development. An example of this is evident when considering some of Erikson's (1968) concepts related to psychosocial growth. He suggested that individuals pass through eight interrelated stages. During the first or second year of life, parental nurturing and care determine if a child trusts or mistrusts others. The second stage occurs between eighteen months and three years. At this point, a child's ability to learn right from wrong influences the level of autonomy or shame experienced. Once a child is then old enough to enter school, issues related to industry and inferiority surface. This is a time when social experiences impact self-esteem. Up until this time, adolescence, skill development was thought to be shaped by what is done to a person. That type of thinking begins to change as teenagers start to contemplate complex issues while simultaneously gaining a sense of empowerment. These newfound feelings of control provide the foundation for seeking intimacy and satisfying relationships as adults. Marriage and child-rearing normally take place at this time in life. As individuals progress into middle age, family and career are the most important aspects of life. Adults work to establish stability and attempt to produce something that makes a difference in society. Inactivity and meaninglessness are common fears during this point in time. Once reaching the final stage in life, significant reflection occurs. Some adults look back with a feeling of integrity while others have a sense of despair (Erikson, 1968).

As Erikson suggested, emotion plays a significant role in the esteem chamber of the tunnel. For example, certain physical characteristics result in particular responses. Attractive individuals usually receive more opportunities than those who are unattractive. This reality of life can be illuminated by reviewing the experiences of Buster and Bob. Buster is a good-looking, well-proportioned youngster whereas Bob is overweight and generally unattractive in the eyes of most. As Buster and Bob enter school, teachers naturally interact with them differently. In most instances, an instinct- based approach-avoidance dichotomy will result in Buster gaining more attention, guidance, and support than Bob. As Buster and Bob become older, an emotion-based confounding effect will impact how each feel in relationship to strength, status, confidence, and level of respect gained from others. What is also evident is how Bob and many others are conditioned to believe that they can and should do certain things to become more physically attractive. For example, a makeover consisting of a new hairstyle, wardrobe, and dental work would help them feel better about themselves. This type of thinking may explain why most television executives, movie producers, and advertisers rely on those perceived as attractive to convey information. It too may be the reason why billions of dollars each year are spent on exercise equipment, diets, and plastic surgery.

Another less obvious indoctrinated belief is the connection between esteem and education level. The higher the degree, the more status someone is thought to receive. This idea results in an education system in which individuals spend significant amounts of money, time, and energy attempting to gain credentials symbolizing the ability to perform certain tasks. What is also evident is that some disciplines receive higher status than others.

If someone is a medical doctor or lawyer, they are thought of and often treated differently than business owners, educators, and law enforcement officers. These differences as well are reflected in the level of compensation received. What is perhaps unknown or forgotten is that many entrepreneurs and those with significant wealth have rejected some of the indoctrinated beliefs associated with the link between formal education and success. It too is virtually impossible to explain how some individuals, regardless of ability, seem to be in the right place at the right time to gain opportunities others do not receive.

What is also noticed in the esteem chamber of the tunnel is that most adults appear conditioned to live in a "whirlwind," striving to obtain something of perceived value. This pattern of behavior often creates feelings of despair, withdrawal, and a sense of hopelessness and helplessness in which individuals view themselves as static, limited, expendable, and estranged. To offset and perhaps even escape these negative feelings, information is often sought and believed without proof or evidence to the contrary. Adults who demonstrate these thoughts and actions naturally are more likely to regress or become stuck in lower chambers of the tunnel. However, if adults are not concerned with what others might think, they may increase their sense of esteem and general quality of life. A simplistic example occurs when a couple decides to complete a fourteen-day automobile trip from Gainesville, Florida, to San Francisco, California. They decide to initially drive north toward Chicago, Illinois, stopping along the way to visit various historical landmarks prior to traveling west. As one might expect, it will take them more time and resources to reach San Francisco; nevertheless, veering from the traditional path resulted in a journey that was memorable and enjoyable. If individuals literally and figuratively travel on nontraditional paths, they may experience self-actualization.

SELF-ACTUALIZATION CHAMBER

Adults in the self-actualization chamber of the tunnel participate in an ongoing process in which their abilities are fully, creatively, and joyfully utilized (Maslow, 1971). They understand themselves, not only in terms of their mission in life but why they like certain foods, friends, and activities. Maslow identified eight specific behaviors that these individuals typically exhibit:

(1) concentration—experiencing daily activities fully, vividly, selflessly, with total absorption, (2) growth—willingness to take calculated risks rather than relying on safe predictable patterns of behavior, (3) Self-awareness—becoming more conscious of the inner self, (4) honesty—taking responsibility for your behavior rather than attempting to please others or to enhance your own status, (5) judgment—trusting your own feelings and acting accordingly, (6) self-development—exploring one's potential by living, working, and relating to the world rather than to a single event or accomplishment, (7) peak experiences— identifying periods of time when feelings, thoughts, and actions are clear and accurate, (8) lack of ego defenses—recognizing how certain feelings distort images of people and events (Maslow, 1971). If, and when individuals collectively demonstrate the aforementioned actions, they progress toward and perhaps reach the self-actualization chamber of the tunnel.

The features of self-actualization are influenced by emotion-based variables. One example is the manner in which appropriate responses are determined. In most instances, a quantitative point of view establishes and governs what is acceptable and unacceptable behavior. This bell-shaped curve approach considers normal behavior as that which 68 percent (one standard deviation above or below the mean) of the population exhibit. Those who demonstrate actions varying from the majority often create discomfort in others, are labeled, and thought in need of certain types of intervention. Evidence of this is often associated with the use of the *Diagnostic Statistical Manual*. This attempt to describe, define, and standardize human actions seems to create an atmosphere that limits the likelihood of obtaining self-actualization. As a result, limited models of self-actualization might be present, and those who are may be portrayed as different, scary, hard to be around, and perhaps even dangerous.

It also appears that emotion more so than intellect determines the number of adults in the self-actualization chamber. More specifically, episodic or long-term periods of lack of need fulfillment lessens the likelihood of obtaining self-actualization. An example might be captured in a life timeline. Initially, when an infant is born, their basic needs are met; then at eighteen months of age, they experience a temporary lack of need fulfillment. For most, innate resiliency results in little or no harm. However, if this pattern continues during childhood and adolescents, a confounding effect may lessen the probability of obtaining self-actualization. Another emotion -based variable is the speed and ongoing pace in which adults live. This aspect of life can be described along a continuum beginning with a "log" ending with a "whirlwind." A log represents limited purpose-driven actions. Adults with this perspective seem to feel they have little control over their experiences as they rely on others to solve problems. In contrast, a whirlwind consists of persistent activity with limited reflection on its value. Those who demonstrate this pattern of behavior appear driven by various traditions and self-imposed standards. One such example are parents who believe children should be involved in as many extracurricular activities as possible; the thought of downtime is not a possibility. In spite of the obvious lifestyle differences between the log and whirlwind, emotion more so than intellect seems to determine the likelihood of someone experiencing self-actualization.

A greater understanding of the intellectual self may help to increase the number of adults in the self-actualization chamber of the tunnel. The intellectual self is comprised of a basic level of literacy, interpersonal skills, problem-solving abilities, and a learning opportunity personal perspective. Collectively, these components allow someone to easily navigate their environment. An example is an individual who is able to identify past events that trigger certain feelings associated with the current experience. Once recognized, changes in basic physiological responses such as adrenalin level, skin tone, and heart rate are understood as normal events. Then after a brief period of time, a sense of empowerment may allow them to contemplate a variety of problem-solving options. Another possible way to increase the amount time in the intellectual self is to identify and determine how past experiences shape identity. This type of self-investment will result in a variety of emotions such as anger, happiness, sadness, and disillusionment. Once an issue is emotionally experienced and thought about, it seems logical that individuals will have an increased likelihood of obtaining self-actualization. For most, the consistent use of the intellectual self results in the energy needed to promote concentration, growth, self-awareness, honesty, and judgment. It too will help identify peak experiences, ego defenses, and desirable areas of self-development.

SUMMARY OF THE TUNNEL'S CHAMBERS

Maslow's (1968) hierarchy of needs provides the structure to organize and discuss how emotion presents itself within the tunnel. It appears that individuals have been and always will be dependent on others to fulfill physiological, safety, belonging and love, and esteem needs. This aspect of the human condition explains why indoctrination exists and will continue throughout time. It also seems difficult and perhaps impossible for many to reach self-actualization without a significant sense of empowerment.

Nevertheless, individuals do have daily opportunities to think about why certain information is considered to be true without question or despite evidence to the contrary. If adults would reflect upon this aspect of life, they may become more aware of how their emotions impact their experiences. This enhanced level of self-awareness might help them expend energy in ways that ultimately result in increased feelings of empowerment and a level of emotional calmness. In some instances, opportunities may even arise to alter the method and content in which future generations are indoctrinated.

CHANGING THE METHOD AND CONTENT OF INDOCTRINATION

Altering the method or content of indoctrination begins with an awareness of an alternative viewpoint. In most instances, if the concept challenges traditional beliefs, instinctive responses act as protective barriers to discredit not only the suggestion but also the individual proposing it. The emotions experienced at that particular point in time typically results in a certain level of energy available to determine the idea's merits. What is also evident and perhaps important to consider is that the longer a principle has existed and more concrete it is, the more likely it will remain a part of the indoctrination process. A brief discussion of global warming and college football may clarify this observation.

Global warming is the belief that the earth's atmosphere and ocean temperature is rising (Sachs, 2008). Pelham (2009) indicated that the average temperature increased by 1.33 degrees Fahrenheit during the twentieth century. He further suggested that it will continue to rise somewhere within the range of 2.7 to 11 degrees Fahrenheit in the next century. If this happens, sea levels will become higher, precipitation patterns will change, and the subtropical deserts will expand. Other likely effects include more frequent extreme weather events, such as heat waves, droughts, and flash flooding (Pelham, 2009). In spite of the significant evidence indicating that the earth's surface temperature has increased, one third of the world's population is unaware of global warming (Pelham, 2009). A number of reasons have been presented as to why individuals have limited knowledge. The most obvious is that the phrase is relatively new; it did not surface until approximately 1975 (Broecker, 1975). Still, even when adults have been exposed to the concept, many may not understand it due to the terms used or the complexities associated with it. Another possible explanation is that the consequences of global warming are not perceived as directly impacting daily life. It seems relatively obvious, then, that ideas initially have to enter human consciousness and be understood before they will be considered of value and worthy of dissemination.

College football in the state of Alabama is another example of the challenges associated with altering the method and content of indoctrination. In most instances, residents are indoctrinated to be fans of Auburn University or the University of Alabama. This allegiance begins at birth with some parents naming their child after their favorite coach or player while dressing their infant in orange and blue or red and white. As children become older, life experiences not only strengthen their emotional attachment to their parents and grandparents but also to their family's chosen school. As these shared emotion-laden football experiences unfold, some children and adults appear to link a part of their identity with a particular school despite having never attended the institution. This perspective is not only reflected in tattoos, license plates, and in personal conversations, but how adults spend limited resources on game tickets, memorabilia, and support exorbitant coach's salaries and stadium expansions. After reflecting upon this aspect of life in Alabama, what would have to occur for people to alter the emphasis placed on college football? The logical answer is discomfort and pain.

Discomfort is defined as a multifaceted response to environmental stimuli that creates emotional or physiological disequilibrium. This disharmony results in various sensations that impact how someone perceives themselves and their immediate environment. Granted, discomfort is a part of the human experience; however, at some point, individual and collective discomfort becomes perceived as pain. Once this moment is reached, opportunities may exist to alter the method and content of indoctrination. To quantify this idea, a discomfort continuum could possibly be designed consisting of a cardinal scale beginning with one ending at ten. One would indicate little emotional or physical uneasiness; ten represents life-threatening violent acts. Points between these extremes represent the level of discomfort present. When using this type of metric, it might be possible to suggest that the more frequent and extreme an action is, the more likely it will result in some degree of change.

A threat of harm or act of violence appears to be the only expedient way to alter the method and content of indoctrination. In the 1980s for example, information regarding acquired immune deficiency syndrome (AIDS) led to an increased awareness and use of universal precautions. Individuals in many disciplines are now trained to use latex gloves as protective barriers to bodily fluids. Even when observing sporting events, if blood is present, athletic trainers immediately "glove up" prior to interacting with the athlete. The aftermath of September 11, 2001, provides further evidence of how extreme events promote change. In the United States, a rekindling of patriotism led to the purchase and flying of American flags and increased participation in various religious activities. Citizens as well seemed more than willing to sacrifice personal liberties in the name of safety. For instance, airline travelers are now conditioned to believe that they have to arrive at least two hours prior to departure in order to pass through various security measures. Most passengers, without question, comply with policies that require them to remove their shoes and other personal items. These changes to some degree create a new standard of behavior. Other historical examples of how a threat of harm or violence changed the indoctrination content may be uncovered when studying the events surrounding world wars and the Great Depression.

CHAPTER SUMMARY

This chapter demonstrated how emotion is reflected and captured within the human indoctrination process. Indoctrination was defined and discussed in the context of daily living. A number of variables were presented to describe how children and adults are influenced to believe information without proof or evidence to the contrary. Topics explored included religious beliefs, personal relationships, communication patterns, and the rule of law. Emotion was presented as the reason why indoctrination seems to happen without an awareness that it is occurring. The emotions experienced within the indoctrination process is also thought to result in an imbalance of power; certain individuals or groups shape the method and content in which children and adults are indoctrinated.

A tunnel example was then used to describe the indoctrination process. Its dimensions represented the mores and values of society and average life expectancy. Human emotion was suggested as the reason why the tunnel exists and individuals enter and remain. It was also noted that adults who temporarily leave the tunnel often return because of the emotional responses of their spouses, family, and friends. For those who do permanently exit, they are often perceived as deficit, labeled, and in need of ongoing supervision. Another observation presented was how the dimensions of the tunnel act paradoxically. The width and length provide the sense of order needed for some to identify and nurture their talent; while for others, it acts to oppress innate ability. Maslow's (1968) ideas were then used to represent the specific chambers of the tunnel. After exploring the many complexities associated with the physiological, safety, love and belonging, esteem, and self-actualization chambers, it was clear that emotion is the reason why individuals are easily led, influenced, and not really in control of their own fate. This aspect of the human experience explains why indoctrination has been and always will be a constant within the tunnel. It was also suggested that at any point in time, opportunities exist to determine why certain information is considered to be true without question or despite evidence to the contrary. If individuals would reflect upon this aspect of life, they possibly could become more aware of how their emotions impact their daily experiences. This enhanced level of self-awareness may ultimately help them expend energy in ways that result in a sense of empowerment and a higher quality of life.

To conclude the chapter, a few thoughts were presented on how emotion more so than intellect is the catalyst for altering the method and content of indoctrination. This pattern of events typically begins with an awareness of an alternative viewpoint. Then, instinctive self- preservation responses to some degree not only discredit the idea but also the individual proposing it. In some cases, if the concept challenges traditional beliefs, emotion lessens or perhaps even depletes the energy required to determine the idea's merits. What is also evident is that the longer a principle has existed and more concrete it is, the more likely it will remain a part of the indoctrination process. It was also discussed how the logical catalyst for change is discomfort and pain. Ideas related to a discomfort continuum were presented to calculate the probability in which the method and content of indoctrination might change. It was concluded that the emotions associated with a threat of harm or act of violence will continue to be the only expedient way to significantly alter the method and content of indoctrination.

To think further about why broad societal changes do not occur, it might be helpful to explore how communication acts as the medium of emotion. That is the topic of the upcoming chapter.

COMMUNICATION:
THE MEDIUM OF EMOTION

Broad societal changes do not happen because the core of human beings, emotion and intellect, is impossible to significantly alter. Emotion more so than intellect, ultimately influences and determines what individuals hear, view, and do. This reality of life is evident when considering how individuals communicate with each other. As messages are received, corresponding ideas are triggered, formulated, and disseminated. This evolving dynamic provides the foundation for need fulfillment and determines the general quality of life. Naturally, the emotions within and associated with these interactions filter and shape how messages are conveyed and understood and corresponding actions are exhibited. With this aspect of the human experience in mind, this chapter will explore how human emotion impacts communication patterns that promote or hinder the probability of individual and collective change. Please note, at no time does the author claim to have a definitive answer for how individuals or groups should communicate. However, thinking about communication might result in interesting discoveries that improve the quality of life.

Initially, the role of emotion in everyday activities is discussed.

EMOTION

Emotion consists of complex layers of processes that are in constant contact with the environment. At a minimum, these interactions include cognitive stimuli appraisal or evaluation of meaning and physical changes such as endocrine, autonomic, and cardiovascular. Emotion is the energy that drives, organizes, amplifies, and attenuates cognitive activity within the socially influenced value- appraising process of the brain (Siegel, 1999). Emotions range from primitive reflexes and responses to multifaceted complexities labeled and described as happiness, anger, joy, sadness, guilt, fear, hope, and love. These internal feelings vary for each individual and present themselves on a frequency and intensity continuum ranging from no response to rage and violence. Initially, this is reflected in a baby's cry for comfort and ultimately ends at the mourning of life. In between these periods, verbal and nonverbal communication patterns reflect the varying degrees of emotion present in each experience.

When language appeared between thirty thousand and one hundred thousand years ago, gestures were used to communicate the emotions related to basic survival instincts (Pinker, 2007, 2002, and 1995). As time passed, individuals within certain cultures refined how they stood or moved while simultaneously associating sounds with certain objects or actions. For example, when an animal approached, a tribal leader may have uttered a noise that later was shaped and modified based on previous usage and context. Ultimately, sequences of sounds became associated with an object, such as the word *deer* used to label a brown animal with antlers capable of running and jumping. Variations of sounds also naturally arose from the larynx. These modifications resulted from the fact that sounds are broken when in contact with the uvula and the sides of the tongue in the throat, against the palate or the teeth, and through contact with the lips (Khaldun, 2005). Oral language patterns as well continually evolve as new discoveries result in a variety of words and phrases to describe objects, functions, and theories (McWhorter, 1998). Today, Harrub, Thompson, and Miller (2003) state that by the age of six, most youth learn to use and understand about thirteen thousand words, and by eighteen, they will have a working vocabulary of sixty thousand words. Children learn on average a new word every ninety minutes of their waking life. In spite of the amount of words acquired, understood, and used, emotion more so than intellect shapes the content and manner in which people communicate.

As new disciplines form and develop, nomenclatures are also created. These systems of terms begin with an idea or the discovery of some phenomenon followed by a systematic process of definition, discussion, acceptance, and dissemination. An example is the field of special education. Special education formally began in the United States in 1975 with the passage of Public Law 94- 142: The Education for All Handicapped Children Act (Turnbull, Turnbull, Shank, and Leal, 2010). Public schools are now required to provide a free and appropriate education to children who were previously denied formal schooling. As these initial legal requirements were interpreted and implemented, professionals defined the population of interest using terms such as learning disabilities, autism, orthopedic handicaps, and serious emotional disturbance. As time passed, ongoing debate led to changes in terminology and intervention strategies. For instance, the term "mental retardation" evolved to "intellectual disabilities." Once general terminology is agreed upon, research is then usually conducted to determine the extent certain methodology results in desired outcomes. It appears that regardless of the discipline, labeling and categorizing entities provides the sense of order needed to promote communication, organization, formal training, and the allocation of resources.

EMOTION AND COMMUNICATION: PROMOTING INTIMACY AND DIVISION

The quality of one's life is influenced by the extent in which emotion shapes personal interactions. To gain a greater understanding of this idea, a continuum labeled survival to enlightenment might be helpful. Survival represents emotion-based interpretations of environmental stimuli; enlightenment reflects intellectual-based perceptions. Adults, to some degree, innately function closer to survival rather than enlightenment regardless of their economic status, education level, and material possessions. Granted, there are various subtleties and points along the continuum, the impact of emotion on communication patterns appear everywhere as a social constant. For example, the primitive need for safety explains why some adults struggle with living alone and silence. Many appear constantly afraid as they purchase security systems or have the television on for noise. One person recently stated, "Television acts as company, causing me to forget that I am in the house by myself." Another less obvious action sometimes occurs as children and adults interact with each other. Words or phrases (fillers) are frequently inserted to avoid pauses within a conversation; momentary silence appears to create a sense of uneasiness. Collectively, these emotion-based responses seem to act paradoxically, as protection, while simultaneously lessening emotional intimacy.

Communication patterns naturally shape relationships. A sense of closeness or uneasiness usually develops between individuals as they share experiences. It seems logically then that the extent and quality of interaction is influenced by a person's frame of reference at a particular point in time. In most instances, if someone is physically tired or is reminded of an individual they dislike, they may not hear what is said. However, if they express ideas similar to the listener, they are more likely to continue the discussion. Another example of emotion's role in communication is noticed when someone has recently been divorced. Past relationship difficulties often cause them to place protective barriers around themselves in order to obtain a sense of psychological safety. What is also evident is that even within long-term relationships, adults struggle developing the boundaries essential to obtain and maintain harmony and understanding.

Emotion impacts the ability to understand verbal messages. When children and adults encounter stimuli creating discomfort, they sometimes misinterpret information while demonstrating a variety of patterns of behavior. As these responses develop and evolve, an approach- avoidance dichotomy shapes the type, frequency, and context of future experiences. An example is how some adults react to those who have multiple body piercing and tattoos. In some instances, they become intellectually paralyzed with the question, "Why would anyone do that to their body?" As this occurs, they may miss the opportunity to interact with someone that could positively alter their life. This pattern of avoidance and lack of understanding can be traced to the self-preservation fear response.

Even with a shared language, emotion may cause limited understanding. An example sometimes occurs when United States citizens travel to the United Kingdom. The environment feels different because the sounds present are unusual as variations in voice tone, word selection, and rate of verbal output make it hard at times to follow and comprehend ongoing conversations. This sense of disconnection and resulting uneasiness may be similar to what happens when someone is invited to a party in which they do not know anyone. Upon arriving, the guest instinctively gravitates toward an individual or group that may have similar life experiences. As one would too expect, differences in native language limit understanding. Translating words from one language to another results to some degree in a loss of intended meaning. Information is shared; yet, depth of understanding may be compromised due to subtle variations in voice tone, inflection, and word meaning.

Communication is also nonverbal. The standing position, eye contact, and body movement either promote or hinder the comprehension of the oral message. Two questions naturally arise when thinking about nonverbal communication. How do nonverbal communication patterns develop, and in what ways do they differ based on culture, gender, geographic region, socioeconomic level, and education? Despite attempts to answer the aforementioned questions, limited quantitative and qualitative evidence seems to exist. It perhaps may not be scientifically possible to determine with any degree of confidence the evolving nature of emotion and its impact on verbal and nonverbal communication patterns. However, based on daily observations, emotion provides the foundation for the content and interpretation of most nonverbal messages. Some adults, for instance, convey their emotions by "wearing them on their sleeves" while others are despondent almost void of emotion. In between these extremes, the vast majority of individuals communicate nonverbally in ways that allow them to fulfill their basic personal needs. The ability to interpret the nonverbal messages of others is also impacted by emotion. Emotionally distraught individuals have limited ability to identify and interpret nonverbal actions. In some instances, nonverbal communication will have to become more direct and perhaps verbal in order for understanding to occur.

In summary, emotion appears to divide individuals from each other rather than promoting high levels of personal intimacy. It too appears that as uneasiness arises, most adults attempt to obtain safety and security by labeling and categorizing environmental stimuli. This innate pattern of behavior may explain why peace accords between nations, and statements such as "Can't we all get along?" have minimal success. The need for acceptance is another possible reason as to why emotion divides rather than promotes closeness between people. This ongoing quest for belonging or "fitting in" begins at birth and continues throughout life as individuals usually adopt the behavior of their parents or others around them. Emotion, rather than intellect, also provides a logical reason why individuals spend limited time attempting to communicate with those who are different from them.

EMOTIONS ROLE IN COMMUNICATION

To frame the discussion of emotion's role in communication, specific elements will be discussed individually and then collectively. Readers should not infer that the author believes that it is possible to simplify communication into six categories; however, it is one way to think about a complex evolving dynamic. Communication components to be considered include: (1) thoughts and ideas, (2) word selection, (3) nonverbal messages, (4) listening, (5) memory, and (6) recall and use.

EMOTION, THOUGHTS AND IDEAS

Emotion impacts thoughts, ideas, and the ability to learn. Children and adults have limited capacity to acquire, store, and retain information when they are concerned about a loved one, job loss, pending expense, or other similar issue. This episodic turmoil, for some, becomes a way of life as emotion more so than intellect governs perception and action. Phrases such as, "Timing is everything" and "You have to wait until they are in a good mood to tell them" bare this out. Emotions impact on learning is also evident when you consider how individuals obtain information. Children acquire many responses simply by watching and listening to those around them (Bandura, 1977). For instance, the baby who claps her hands after her mother, the child who angrily hits a playmate in the same way they have been punished at home, and the teenager who wears the same clothes and hairstyle as their friends are all displaying observational learning. It seems logical then that when an individual is emotionally distressed, they are less likely to observe or correctly interpret what is happening around them. The intensity and length of time in discomfort may as well determine how decisions promote or hinder innate potential. An example might be someone who copes with negative emotions by shopping or eating. Temporary comfort is gained; however, long-term consequences may ultimately hinder future opportunities.

Emotion guides most ideas. This aspect of the human condition may explain why a level of mistrust seems to permeate individual interactions. For instance, ongoing questions and skepticism regarding personal motivations can be traced to the basic need for survival and ongoing desire for a sense of safety. As adults attempt to protect themselves, they seem to become insulated with certain thoughts and ideas while congregating with others who have similar beliefs. It too appears that in order for a new idea to become accepted, individuals in positions of authority have to communicate the concept or the information has to be repeated a certain number of times. As this dissemination process unfolds, the amount of information acquired is determined based on the emotional state in which someone is in at the moment or the feelings generated from the topic.

Genetics, coupled with the human indoctrination process, explains why intuition rather than science guides most ideas. Beginning at birth, a young child's actions reflect the emotional support needed to feel a sense of attachment and belonging. As time passes, communication patterns become more sophisticated, evolving from a cry to seeking and gaining wisdom from an elderly relative. While this normal pattern of behavior unfolds, little emphasis is naturally placed on science. It further appears then that when emotion governs most thoughts and actions, individuals assume certain observations, facts, and theories are true without question. Assumptions, in many instances, fulfill the immediate emotional need for order and safety. In contrast, scientific principles often create a sense of uneasiness by uncovering and detailing information that challenge the legitimacy of long standing beliefs.

The emotions associated with reinforcement also shape thoughts and ideas. If an action results in positive reinforcement, similar behaviors are repeated. An example is noticed when an employee of an acoustic business uncovers an alternative strategy to grid a ceiling. If the owner positively recognizes the innovation, he will be more prone in the future to think about alternative strategies. In contrast, if the employer responds negatively, he will be less likely to venture from standard operating procedures. Other questions that might highlight the significance of reinforcement include the following: Would a politician be reelected if they presented ideas the majority did not agree with? Would an athlete be perceived as a professional if they were unable to hit a baseball or tennis ball, shoot a basket, run fast, or kick a soccer ball? Another less obvious example is how adults are treated when their thoughts differ from the majority. In some historical accounts, scholars and innovators were thought of as mentally retarded because their ideas made those around them uncomfortable.

A common response pattern sometimes surfaces when an idea is presented that creates discomfort. Adults normally respond as though they are shocked while wondering, "Did they really say that?" or "Did I hear them incorrectly?" If the individual repeats what was previously expressed, they often are ignored, avoided, or labeled a troublemaker, know-it-all, or other similar negative word or phrase. As this typical communication dynamic unfolds, those who are unable to interpret nonverbal messages are more likely to be treated differently or denied opportunities. An example is a nontenured professor who is capable but loses creditability because of a lack of social skills. Despite a strong desire to teach, after seven years, she is unable to maintain her position as a professor. Not only do individuals struggle with those who are perceived as insensitive, they also seek activities that will distract them from emotional discomfort. This desire may explain why leisure activities are valued and entertainers such as athletes or actors are compensated at exorbitant levels. What is further apparent is that some individuals search for something that will provide them with emotion-based stimulation. Evidence of this might be found in popular television shows such as the *Biggest Loser*, *Survivor*, rap music, or other commercially produced activities that attempt to push the envelope related to free speech, sex, and obscenity (Postman, 1985). It seems relatively clear that as individuals attempt to escape emotional discomfort, they often think and act in ways to fulfill their immediate needs.

In summary, emotion acts as the catalyst and energy for ideas. Without a sense of urgency, many discoveries may not have happened. In spite of what might be thought of as resulting in collective benefit, most thoughts and actions seem self-serving often reflecting attempts to meet short rather than long-term needs.

As individuals seek to fulfill their immediate needs and desires, genetic and experiential differences result in varying abilities to develop original ideas, conceptualize how multiple thoughts are connected, and understand how certain ideas promote or hinder long-term outcomes. Despite a shared system of formal communication, variations in individual emotional responses appear to impact the development and understanding of ideas.

EMOTION AND WORD SELECTION

Traditions, along with recent practice, guide word selection. If certain terms result in positive feelings or outcomes, they will be repeated in other contexts. Words are not void of emotion but rather reflect the various sensations experienced within families, places of worship, schools, and neighborhoods. Evidence of this is noticed when you consider how certain slang or types of dialect are used to convey information. For example, regional differences in the United States explain why it is common to hear the word *soda* expressed in Alabama and *pop* in Minnesota. Other such variations are found in phrases such as "It is flooding over here," or "I carried him to the store."

Children and adults use certain words to convey meaning based on how they feel at a particular point in time. Words seem to reflect three distinct categories: (1) neutral, (2) positive, and (3) negative. Neutral words consist of *such, how, as, when, where, is, begin, after, daily*, and certain names of objects. A sample of positive terms may include *helpful, happy, benefit, advantage, significant, wonderful, splendid, overcome, colorful*, and *abundant*. Negative terminology could be *sorry, sad, problem, harm, disillusionment, overwhelmed, depressed, frightened*, and *troubled*.

Children and adults appear to select words consciously or subconsciously that simultaneously reflect their immediate emotions and core values. As this occurs, self-preservation (physical survival and protection of ego), in whatever form it presents itself, governs word choices.

The emotions associated with words and phrases result in varying levels of understanding or confusion. For example, the popular statement, "It is what it is," seems to be used in a multitude of ways implying various meanings. For some, it might act as a way to escape or cope with a difficult situation, while others might pay limited attention or even laugh at the statement. Phrases such as "Have you picked cotton lately?" or "We are fixin' to go to the store," might also create a variety of unintended emotions for the listener. What is also noticed is that certain words are "emotionally loaded." One such word is *problem*. The term *problem* creates a variety of responses based on the experiences of those participating in the conversation. In certain situations, what is considered a problem could be perceived by others of as an opportunity. It also appears that when adults gain a general awareness of how emotions impact word choices, they are more likely to listen and understand the verbal and nonverbal messages of others.

EMOTION AND NONVERBAL MESSAGES

Emotion is reflected in nonverbal messages. Nonverbal messages range from subtle head and hand movements to looking at your watch or organizing a bag prior to leaving. These actions simultaneously exhibited with verbalizations either promote or hinder understanding. An example is noticed when someone states, "Let me know what I can do to help," while they stand with their arms crossed looking toward the ground. Do they really want to provide assistance, or is this simply a conditioned response that has limited meaning? Nonverbal messages also play an important role in developing intimacy between individuals. When adults perceive that someone is intently listening and cares about their experiences, they sense that they are of value or worth. This temporary boast in ego and self-esteem seems to promote acceptance and problem solving. In contrast, if nonverbal messages are misinterpreted, they often act as barriers to further dialogue. In extreme cases, anger may result from the frustration of not being understood.

An individual's emotional state shapes the content, interpretation, and understanding of nonverbal messages. For example, if an individual is passionate about a particular topic, he seems to increase his voice tone and rate of verbal output while simultaneously exhibiting a higher rate of nonverbal actions. It is also noticed that when adults are in a positive mood, they are more sensitive to the subtle body movements occurring within the communication process. In contrast, if someone is experiencing fear and anxiety, they have difficulties gathering and interpreting information because they are often unable to look beyond their own immediate needs. What is evident as well is that individuals have limited ability to monitor their nonverbal actions when they are feeling a level of physical and emotional discomfort. In some instances, this lack of self-awareness causes them to have difficulties assessing and adapting to the contextual demands of social gatherings and employment settings.

Each culture naturally has a range of acceptable nonverbal behavior. The parameters of which are determined and shaped by the emotional reactions individuals have to certain behavior. For example, placing a finger in an orifice or using a certain hand to perform a basic need would be perceived as inappropriate in some civilizations. When you further reflect on nonverbal behavior, some actions trigger limited emotional response. A possible explanation for this is the frequency in which a behavior is exhibited. The more often something occurs, the greater likelihood it becomes the norm. With this thought in mind, nonverbal actions seem to be exhibited with little thought and are remembered only when they are beyond the parameters of the adopted cultural standards.

EMOTION AND LISTENING

Listening ranges from reacting to a loud noise to determining the subtle variations in sounds of birds and musical instruments. It goes beyond the ability to hear as it attempts to gain meaning from stimuli within the environment. Skills, such as, concentration, patience, and memory determine the extent and quality of listening. When individuals are thinking about something other than what is currently occurring, they are more likely to hear a limited amount of information. For instance, if a father and his young daughter encounter someone from high school while in the grocery store, the extent and quality of interaction will often be determined by the ability to concentrate. At that moment, if he is experiencing a sense of time constraints or another emotion-based thought, he is less likely to participate and remember the interaction. Adults, who are excellent listeners, appear to possess an internal state of calmness that allows them to monitor and sometimes block emotion-based thoughts. This state of being seems to correlate with levels of self-awareness. When one is aware of and understands their own emotions, they are more likely to develop the level of self-control and sense of harmony needed to acquire, interpret, and remember information.

Patience is another important variable in listening. It is thought of as the ability to tolerate delay, provocation, and annoyance without complaint or anger (Webster, 1993) . In some instances, when someone experiences a difficult feeling, they have limited patience and sensitivity to those around them. Impatience appears to manifest and present itself as impulsivity. Granted, genetics impacts impulsivity; however, it also reflects a response to an emotion- based need. An example might be noticed in statements such as "There is just not enough time in the day to get everything done that needs to be done," or "I could work around the clock, and it really would not matter." This sense of helplessness might reflect how emotion colors someone's ability to develop the level of patience needed to gain information from the environment.

Memory skills essential for listening are also impacted by emotion. In most instances, environmental events trigger past thoughts that either promote or hinder the acquisition of information. It appears that stimuli entering short - and long-term memory is determined based on the depth of emotion associated with certain experiences. For example, if someone feels they have been harmed in some way by their parents, friends, teachers, or employer, they are more likely to recall the exact events. In contrast, if a pleasant experience occurred at the grocery store, they are less likely to remember what specifically happened. Another example of emotion's role in listening is noticed when individuals interpret stimuli differently in a shared experience. Emotional responses to voice tone, pitch, rate, color, texture, and nonverbal messages may account for the variations in what is heard, understood, and remembered.

The dynamics of a conversation illustrate the role of emotion in listening. For example, a discussion consists of two or a group of individuals voluntarily engaged with each other. Initially, a thought is stated verbally; others, then, respond or convey subtle nonverbal cues that they are not interested in the subject. If the discourse though continues, when someone experiences a sense of uneasiness, they gradually become less capable of hearing and listening to what is being said. In extreme cases, an emotion-based reaction may create a barrier, or wall, between participants. The depth of conversation is also often determined by the amount of emotional intimacy felt between individuals. If a certain level of closeness exists, the dialogue has a greater likelihood of continuing; if not, participants seem hesitant, afraid to hurt the feelings of others, or they verbally discredit the information conveyed. An adult's emotional response to certain topics seems to act as an invisible boundary that promotes or hinders the ability to listen.

What is heard and remembered in a group situation is often determined by emotion. In most instances, emotion creates a hierarchical structure where certain individuals are heard and others are not. For example, adults who are perceived as having "the ear of the boss" are treated differently than those who do not. Within most groups, alliances are naturally formed in order to lessen the sense of uneasiness felt participating in collaborative activities. What is also sometimes noticed is how certain individuals shape the conversation by the quantity of information shared. An adult, who is a person of few words, gains power because they rarely speak; someone who continually talks often is paid little attention. It seems clear that the emotions of group members coupled with the feelings generated during shared experiences determine the extent and quality of listening.

Three outcomes seem to result from emotions impact on listening. The most obvious is that partial amounts of information are gained. When adults obtain limited pertinent facts, they are more likely to rely on intuitive thought rather than science to guide their actions. An example is noticed with some parents of children with autism spectrum disorders. They are willing to spend large amounts of money on unproven intervention strategies, such as special diets or swimming with dolphins, in an attempt to help their child. Another outcome of emotions impact on listening is how people respond to certain individuals. Talented and respected entertainers, such as Oprah Winfrey, Charles Barkley, Sean Penn, Dennis Quaid, Bono, and George Clooney, seem to have the opportunity to shape public opinion in spite of having limited formal training and direct experience with their issue of concern. Lastly, when adults struggle with listening, they appear more likely to experience fear. In some instances, misinterpretations of media content change the daily activities of life. For example, accounts of plane crashes cause some to declare that they will drive their car rather than fly. In actuality, individuals are more likely to experience harm on the highway rather than in the sky. Another lifestyle-altering example occurred when a popular magazine labeled a group of young people "super-predators without a conscience." Some adults are now afraid to shop at night because they are conditioned to believe that a teenager might be lurking, preparing to rob them.

EMOTION AND MEMORY

Information-processing theory provides the foundation to consider emotion and memory. Three assumptions guide this approach (Searleman and Herrmann, 1994). Information is processed in distinct stages beginning with attending to a stimulus, followed by recognition, transformation into mental representation, comparisons with data existing in memory, assigning meaning, and acting in some fashion. Second, there are limits on how much information can be processed at each stage. Although the absolute amount individuals can learn appears to be limitless, it must be acquired gradually. Third, the human information-processing system is interactive. Information stored in memory influences and is influenced by perception and attention. Individuals are thought to observe what prior experiences direct them to see, and what is seen affects what they know (Searleman and Herrmann, 1994). Additionally, innate control processes such as attention, encoding, and maintenance interact simultaneously to determine the type and quantity of information stored and retrieved from memory.

The sensory register acts as the first memory store (Snowman, McCown, and Biehler, 2009). Its purpose is to hold information one to three seconds for children and adults to decide whether they want to further attend. This process of unending series of sounds and instant- camera snapshots each last a brief moment before fading away. When an individual recognizes and thinks about one of the sounds or images, it will be processed and transferred to short- term memory. Short term-memory holds approximately seven unrelated bits of information for twenty seconds and is referred to as working memory (Hambrick and Engle, 2003). Data is then transferred to long-term memory if a certain number of maintenance and elaborative rehearsal activities occur. Long-term memory is unlimited; it contains a permanent record of everything an individual has learned (Schunk, 2004). This store of knowledge is usually organized in abstract structures summarizing aspects of life experiences. When these schemata are well formed and a specific event is consistent with expectations, comprehension occurs. If poorly structured or absent, learning is slow and uncertain (Moreno, 2006).

Emotion is a natural component of memory. As children and adults encounter environmental stimuli, innate responses along with past experiences guide immediate and long-term actions.

A question that naturally arises within this complex dynamic is why certain experiences are remembered and recalled and others are not. The logical answer is that the emotions associated with a given event act to some degree as an imprint on memory. For example, if a child is consistently treated positively, they are more prone to develop an opportunistic life perspective. In contrast, if they are neglected or abused, they appear to struggle with an ongoing sense of fear and anxiety. A possible strategy to quantify how emotion impacts memory might be similar to a common physical pain continuum consisting of a scale of one to ten. The higher the number, the more likely someone needs some form of pharmacological support. While the intervention might provide immediate relief, it also may cause patients to feel they have lost a number of days in their life because they cannot recall the specific events that occurred. What is further noticed is the higher the pain score, the more likely primitive behavior is exhibited, such as the constant need to eat or use the bathroom. Emotional trauma is less noticeable; however, it appears to impact a person's immediate reaction to stimuli and determines what ultimately is observed, heard, and stored in memory.

Memory guides and shapes how individuals communicate. At birth, information from the immediate environment acts as the foundation for the content and manner in which children interact. As youth become older, experiences within their family, places of worship, schools, and neighborhoods impact their developing communication abilities. While this aspect of normal human skill development is unfolding, basic instincts coupled with the need for acceptance are reflected in various patterns of behavior. For instance, a number of adults avoid confrontation in order to gain a sense of belonging. They often appear willing to allow others to treat them negatively until they reach a point where they no longer can tolerate the situation. Another example is noticed with individuals who cannot say no to a request. Refusing to do something seems to result in feelings associated with not being liked. This ongoing desire to be accepted causes some adults to adopt a lifestyle that is not reflective of their hopes, dreams, and desires.

Information stored in memory may also result in an approach-avoidance communication dichotomy. When individuals receive positive verbal and nonverbal feedback, they will continue to interact in similar fashions. If not, they will avoid certain people, situations, and patterns of behavior. A key aspect of this evolving dynamic is the ability to identify and understand the cultural expectations associated with particular contexts. An example is noticed when a young child interrupts their parents conversation. They are reminded to not talk when adults are talking. Another more subtle behavior occurs in an employment setting when an autocratic leader creates an atmosphere of fear and anxiety. Adults seem to isolate themselves or interact with limited numbers of individuals in order to feel insulated from harm. It is also not that uncommon to witness an individual in a grocery store quickly moving to another aisle or acting as though they did not see someone in order to avoid a personal interaction. It appears clear that what is stored in memory is a reflection of the emotions associated with certain experiences. Those feelings, ultimately, determine and influence current and future communication patterns.

EMOTION, RECALL, AND USE

Throughout history, individuals have been indoctrinated by their environment. For example, various scholars have described a hunter-gatherer lifestyle in which children and adults sought the basic necessities of life. As time passed, civilizations have evolved based on food availability, viruses, population migration patterns, and advancements in weaponry (Diamond, 1997). In spite of the many inherent differences in cultures, human emotion and innate intelligence acts as a constant, shaping how children and adults interact with each other. What may also be true is that the human indoctrination process represents or is a result of emotion. For example, the reliance on traditions along with various hierarchical structures seem to provide the sense of ordernecessary to fulfill basic needs, such as food, shelter, and safety. Another consideration is how emotion may promote or hinder the acquisition, storage, recall, and use of information.

Past experiences act as the foundation that guides current and future actions. The emotion-based component of this complex evolving dynamic is reflected in self-esteem. Self-esteem is defined as the overall value or global evaluation individuals make of themselves (Snowman, McCown, and Biehler, 2009). It is sometimes evident in statements such as "I believe that I am an all-right person" and "I am pretty happy with myself." Someone's self-esteem might be thought of along a risk -insulation continuum. If an adult takes calculated chances, they may demonstrate positive self-esteem. Someone who seldom veers from daily routines or acts without thinking might be fearful, impulsive, or stressed with how they feel about themselves. Another possible metric to gauge self-esteem is independent thinking. Adults, who are easily led, void of ideas, or worry about what others might think may struggle with self-esteem. It also appears in some situations that self -esteem coupled with the emotions related to certain memories, result in a sense of urgency. This instinctive response creates a feeling of a lack of control or paralysis in which someone is unable to think about topics other than their immediate concerns. When this occurs, individuals seem more likely to make decisions such as eating or purchasing something to feel better rather than communicating about their difficult experiences.

A number of communication outcomes result when emotion impacts recall and use. The most obvious is that emotions interfere with intellect. Individuals who frequently misinterpret stimuli are more likely to demonstrate actions that reflect immediate rather than long-term thinking. An example in the United States occurred after September 11, 2001. The vast majority of citizens, without question, supported military actions and complied with government safety procedures to offset their fear of terrorists. Another outcome of emotion is associated with the ability to listen. When individuals are participating in a conversation, they seem to instinctively judge and categorize what is heard. As this happens, certain information may not be attended to or stored in short- and long-term memory. Emotion may also promote or hinder the ability to recall information. An example is sometimes noticed when a couple have their first baby. Prior to birth, the parents read a variety of books and talk with others about how to raise children. Yet, once the child is born, emotion rather than intellect seems to govern statements such as "The baby is so little. Do we know how to take care of him? Who will we call if we do not know what to do?"

The frequency and extent of psychological violations also impact the ability to recall and use information. Individuals, as part of the human condition, possess a level of resiliency needed to offset and overcome most emotional difficulties. For some people, however, traumatic experiences result in an inability to retrieve data from memory. An example is sometimes noticed with adults who have been abused. Certain environmental stimuli, such as a smell, sound, or image act as a trigger for a basic physiological self-preservation response. When this occurs, emotion rather than intellect causes them to have limited ability to solve ongoing issues of concern. Additional evidence of this pattern of behavior may be reflected in rates of child neglect, domestic violence, and individual spending habits. It also appears that some adults may become trapped within an emotion-based cycle in which decisions are made that result in ongoing difficulties. Examples are adults who struggle living alone. They seem to cohabitate or marry someone that may not promote their well-being in order to offset their fear of being by themselves. Regrettably, someone who demonstrates this ongoing sequence of events may feel that their life is spiraling out of control.

In summary, the human indoctrination process impacts what information is learned, stored in memory and used in the activities of daily living. Emotion is a major component of this innate process, acting as the catalyst to what is recalled and used. It appears that individuals are innately resilient, able to persevere and overcome most issues of concern. However, if an individual experiences a certain frequency or intensity of emotional violations, they may experience ongoing struggles with self-esteem and the ability to recall and use information.

COLLECTIVE ANALYSIS OF EMOTION AND COMMUNICATION

For communication to occur, there must be shared physical or digital space and a channel of communication existing between individuals. Initially, the sender will convey an idea, perception, or feeling nonverbally and in spoken or written language. The receiver will then interpret the message based on their personal reality. Once meaning has been assigned, a corresponding verbal and nonverbal response is usually emitted. This ongoing sequence of events continues until a participant voluntarily stops talking, walks away, or does not respond to electronic transmissions of information. Successful communication is then thought to have occurred if the perceived message approximates the intent of the sender. In spite of this simplistic linear description, communication is not an absolute finite process. Particularly, communication is often vague and misleading. For example, if the sender says a word such as *closure* or *problem*, she has a certain meaning attached to it in her reality that might not reflect how others perceive the term.

Emotion and intellect are interconnected as individuals communicate. This aspect of the human condition is theoretically impossible to define, delineate, and measure with any level of statistical confidence or certainty. Nevertheless, personal observations and reflections illuminate how emotion more so than intellect acts as the energy that drives, organizes, amplifies, and attenuates how individuals communicate with each other.

Emotion-based actions might be further described and considered along a continuum beginning with primitive reflexes and ending with multifaceted sensations described and labeled as happiness, anger, joy, sadness, guilt, fear, hope, and love. In between these two extremes, genetic and experiential differences may explain the variability in how individuals interact with each other. Additional observation and analysis is warranted to determine the extent of emotions role in thoughts and ideas, word selection, nonverbal messages, listening, memory, and recall and use. Ideally, increased amounts of information and understanding will result in a level of sensitivity needed to increase the probability of individual and collective change.

CHAPTER SUMMARY

Communication is the medium which thoughts and ideas are conveyed. As messages are received, corresponding ideas are triggered, formulated, and disseminated. While this dynamic is evolving and unfolding, layers of emotional processes are generated that filter and shape how information is conveyed, understood, and corresponding actions are exhibited. To further think about this complex aspect of the human condition, a survival to enlightenment continuum was presented. Various nuances, subtleties, and corresponding points along the scale indicate how adults function to some degree within a self-preservation point of view regardless of economic status, education level, and material possessions. It was as well suggested that as discomfort arises, adults persevere and gain comfort by labeling and categorizing environmental stimuli. This innate pattern of behavior coupled with the human indoctrination process may explain why emotion more so than intellect seems to provide the energy for most thoughts while acting paradoxically as a barrier to ideas and depth of understanding.

Specific facets of communication were then discussed to highlight how emotion impacts thoughts and ideas, word selection, nonverbal messages, listening, memory, and recall and use. Emotion is the natural catalyst and energy for most thoughts. Without a sense of urgency, many discoveries would have limited likelihood of occurring. In spite of what others might think of as resulting in collective benefit, most ideas and corresponding actions appear self-serving, reflecting attempts to meet short rather than long -term needs. It was also suggested that variations in genetics and life experiences may explain why adults differ in their ability to understand how emotions promote or hinder immediate and long-term outcomes. The selection and use of words to convey meaning as well reflect the various emotions experienced at a particular moment. Words can be thought of in three distinct categories: (1) neutral, (2) positive, and (3) negative. Neutral words might consist of *such, how, as, when, where, is, beginning, after,* and *daily.* Positive terms may include *helpful, happy, benefit, advantage, significant, wonderful, splendid, overcome, colorful,* and *abundant.* Negative terminology could be *sorry, sad, problem, harm, disillusionment, overwhelmed, depressed, frightened,* and *troubled.*

Nonverbal messages also reflect emotion. When adults notice and are sensitive to the subtle head and hand movements of others, a level of emotional intimacy seems to develop. If nonverbal messages, however, are misinterpreted, barriers to dialogue and relationships develop. It too appears in some instances that individuals have limited ability to monitor their nonverbal actions when they feel emotional and physical discomfort. This lack of self-awareness creates difficulties in assessing and adapting to the contextual demands of social gatherings and employment settings. Emotion is not only present in nonverbal messages, it also results in three common listening outcomes. The most obvious is that partial information is gained. When someone obtains limited pertinent facts, they are more likely to rely on intuitive thought rather than science to guide their actions. Second, the emotions associated with particular individuals seem to determine who shapes public opinion. Talented and respected entertainers often gain a platform to communicate in spite of having limited formal training and direct experience with their issue of concern. Lastly, adults who struggle with listening experience higher levels of fear. Misinterpretations of media content may create feelings of danger that are unwarranted.

An information processing theory was then presented to consider how emotion affects memory. Information is thought to progress in distinct stages, beginning with attending to a stimulus followed by recognition, transformation into mental representation, comparisons with data existing in memory, assigning meaning, and acting in some fashion (Searleman and Herrmann, 1994). This store of data is organized in abstract structures summarizing different cases or examples. When these schemata are well formed and a specific event is consistent with expectations, comprehension occurs. If poorly structured or absent, learning is slow and uncertain (Moreno, 2006) . As this evolving dynamic unfolds, a number of outcomes impact memory, recall, and use. The most obvious is that emotion may interfere or distort the interpretation of stimuli resulting in inappropriate decision making. Another is associated with the ability to listen. Individuals seem to instinctively respond to stimuli by categorizing and judging what is heard. As this occurs, certain information may not be noticed, stored, or recalled from memory.

As the chapter concludes, readers are reminded that the author does not claim to have a definitive answer for how individuals or groups should communicate. Rather, the intent was to stimulate thought on how emotion may act as the energy that drives, organizes, amplifies, and attenuates how individuals communicate with each other. Further observations of individuals interacting with each other are needed to uncover information that might increase the probability of individual and collective change.

THE IMPACT OF EMOTION ON HUMAN DIGNITY

The impetus for this chapter is based on a variety of experiences that have left the author wondering if others consider how their emotions impact human dignity. One memorable example was the medical experiences of Margaret. Margaret is a retired school nurse from New Jersey who currently resides in Florida. When Margaret became older, her mobility is limited by a genetic condition that impacts her hips. For a long time, she has said, "I just have to lose some weight before I have surgery." This statement was an obvious attempt to avoid a fearful experience. Finally, after a number of years struggling to navigate her environment, she decided to have the operation. The events that occurred on the day of her surgery illuminate the complexity of emotion and human dignity.

Margaret's medical procedure was conducted at a major research hospital in Florida. At the hospital that morning, an air of uneasiness permeated around Margaret. Her hands appeared at times to shake, and some of her verbal comments were difficult to comprehend. The hospital staff sensed her discomfort and allowed friends to sit with her in a room adjacent to the surgery area. As we waited, her priest arrived to provide comfort prior to the procedure. While in prayer, two medical professionals came into the room talking, totally oblivious as to what Margaret was experiencing at that particular moment. Their lack of awareness to those around them was difficult to understand. Another disturbing event happened just prior to the surgery; an unfamiliar medical doctor asked Margaret to participate in a pain management research study.

Naturally, she asked a variety of questions that the doctor did not understand or was unwilling to answer. After approximately three minutes of pressuring her to take part in the study, a friend intervened, indicating that she did not want to participate. Why would someone ask Margaret to make an important decision when she was in such an obvious state of emotional turmoil? Following the operation, friends sat with Margaret, waiting for the physical therapist to help her get out of bed and walk. After a number of hours, they arrived, and what followed was troubling. As they began lifting her out of the bed, they did not consider that her back and buttock were not completely covered. When asked to stop and obtain another gown, nonverbally they seemed to communicate that they did not have enough time to do such a thing. Was Margaret simply perceived as a number on a chart they had to work with during their shift? Lastly, the medical professionals did not close the door to Margaret's room prior to helping her walk. With the door open, strangers could view her in state of vulnerability that she had not experienced in over eighty years. Granted, Margaret's experience may not represent what others might encounter; however, other similar examples illuminate the complexities associated with human dignity. Therefore, the purpose of this chapter is to explore how emotion impacts experiences that promote or hinder human dignity. Topics to be explored include the following: (1) "Civility and Human Dignity," (2) "Emotion and Human Dignity," (3) "Acts of Caring: A Means to Measure Emotion and Human Dignity," (4) "Oppression: The Natural Consequence of Emotion on Human Dignity," (5) "Human Responses to Oppression," and (6) "Measuring the Impact of Emotion on Human Dignity."

CIVILITY AND HUMAN DIGNITY

The manner in which people interact is a measure of civility and humanity. Throughout history, wars provide ample evidence of how individuals have struggled with this basic aspect of life. Other less noticeable examples include the general lack of concern among people about events that do not directly affect them and the level of willingness to help others. When further reflecting upon this facet of the human experience, it is important to consider human dignity. Human dignity refers to the highest value or to the presupposition of worth given to people (Lebech, 2004). This theoretical construct is thought to have developed in four distinct stages. Cicero initially explained it on the basis of nature. Thomas Aquinas, who was a part of the Middle Ages' Christocentric perspective, described the concept in relation to Jesus Christ. Immanuel Kant, on behalf of the logocentric framework of modernity, indicated that human dignity was a tribute to reason. Finally, Mary Wollstonecraft representing the polis-centered point of view of postmodernity described human dignity in relation to social acceptability (Lebech, 2004). These four historical accounts coupled with ongoing contemporary dialogue have provided the foundation for the *Universal Declaration of Human Rights* (Lebech, 2004).

The *Universal Declaration of Human Rights* (1948) reflects the transition from high-level philosophical abstractions to more specific actions. Lasswell (1971) noted eight implications from the theoretical construct of dignity:

1. Well-being: the right to life, liberty, and security of person including condemning torture as well as cruel or inhuman treatment and punishment
2. Affection: a person has the right to marry, have a family, and to engage in peaceful assembly and association within a national community
3. Respect: all human beings are born equal in dignity, entitled to all rights and freedoms associated with privacy, family, home, or correspondence
4. Power: the right to take part in the government, to be recognized as a person before the law, and to participate in life within a social and international order
5. Wealth: a right to own property and maintain a standard of living adequate for individual and family well-being
6. Enlightenment: an individual has freedom of opinion and expression, a right to seek, receive and impart information and ideas through the media
7. Skill: the right to education, gainful employment, and opportunities to freely participate in the cultural life of the community
8. Rectitude: affirms an individual's freedom of thought, conscience, and religion

Everyone has a duty to the community, and there is no right to destroy the liberty of others (*Universal Declaration of Human Rights*, 1948). In response to these inalienable rights, the marketplace and public collective actions have become more sensitive to virtually all economic strata, types of persons, groups, and communities with resulting disparities. Some people are simply more fortunate than others. The less-privileged need attention whether they have been identified to participate in special programs or live marginal lives in challenging communities. Despite of what appears to be extensive prior study and dialogue, limited discussions exist today regarding how individual and collective actions affect civility and human dignity.

HUMAN EMOTION AND HUMAN DIGNITY

Human emotion plays a significant role in shaping individual and collective actions that promote or hinder human dignity. Emotions are sensations that naturally occur within a person. They range from primitive reflexes to multifaceted complexities labeled and described as anger, joy, love, and a variety of other terms. Emotion-based behavior is everywhere; it is a societal constant that significantly affects how individuals interact with each other.

ACTS OF CARING: A MEANS TO MEASURE EMOTION AND HUMAN DIGNITY

Acts of caring can be used to determine the extent in which emotion impacts human dignity. Caring is a loving feeling that exhibits concern and empathy for others (Merriam-Webster Online Dictionary, 2009). Watson (1985) suggests that a caring experience occurs when two or more individuals come together in such a way that an occasion for human compassion is possible. She also indicated that acts of caring help someone find harmony in spirit, mind, and body while obtaining meaning in life. These nurturing behaviors could possibly be thought of along a continuum beginning with self- centeredness, unaware of those around you, ending with the loss of life protecting someone else. In between these extremes, human actions perceived as caring are often determined based on a set of contextual and situational specific variables. A recent example occurred in the aftermath of Hurricane Katrina. Many individuals traveling to provide assistance met people who were willing to give whatever money they had to help even though they had limited financial resources. Why did they volunteer to do such a thing when others who have plenty provided only minimal support? Answers to this question and others might help researchers record the specific content and the frequency in which acts of caring are demonstrated.

The type and frequency of acts of caring is normally determined by how someone responds to environmental stimuli. It appears that the intensity of emotional discomfort felt at a particular point in time determines to some degree the probability in which people will help others. Individual genetic variances should also be considered when thinking about emotion and acts of caring. For some adults, their cognitive aptitude results in limited ability to look beyond their own needs. An example of this occurred when a person was in the hospital having back surgery. A long-time friend who had knowledge of the procedure did not visit her and had little contact when she returned home. Recently, the same individual phoned her recovering friend requesting help after a minor medical procedure. Despite her lack of concern for her friend, she expected assistance in her time of need. She is perhaps not selfish but rather has limited insight on how her actions affect those around her. Another important innate variable is associated with perception and interpretation of information. If individuals incorrectly perceive certain colors, textures, and sounds, they sometimes physiologically respond through the emotional frame of reference of "fight or flight." When this happens, decisions are often based on emotion rather than intellect. Adults who frequently state, "I have no other choice," seem to have a sense of hopelessness and a limited ability to demonstrate acts of caring.

The human indoctrination process naturally shapes how emotion affects caring. At the most basic level, children learn to interact with others by observing adults. Usually, if their parents demonstrate caring, they are more likely to exhibit similar patterns of behavior. As youth become older, neighborhood and school experiences either reinforce or negate previously held beliefs. For example, if a student has a series of teachers promoting academic risk taking, they are more likely to learn how their actions impact the plight of those around them. Another conditioned response impacting caring is gender roles. It begins at birth when the color blue is associated with males and pink, females. For most, females rather than males are thought to be more capable of caring and are responsible for nurturing children and adults. This way of thinking is further reflected in vocational choices and female-dominated service leagues. It too appears in some instances that a man's sexuality is questioned when they share their inner most feelings or exhibit emotion in the activities of daily living.

When thinking more about how caring develops, it would be remiss not to consider the role of religion and media. Religion promotes acts of caring. Positive interactions between people are encouraged based on a variety of religious beliefs. Places of worship as well normally act as local community gathering sites consisting of individuals who share a common spiritual perspective to help others. The information conveyed through the media also impact acts of caring. For example, television commercials portraying insects flying and landing on the face of orphaned children seek a heartfelt response. As agency spokespersons state, "For only twenty-four dollars a month, this child will know someone cares about them." The manner and frequency in which the media disseminates information is another feature influencing how individuals think about aspects of their life and the specific behaviors they exhibit.

Acts of caring also evolve and change. For instance, in the United States during the 1960s, government war on poverty programs attempted to provide assistance to those who had limited ability and opportunities. Five decades later, some citizens think the well-intentioned programs promote dependency rather than financial security and empowerment. Some argue that generations of adults today have not experienced the value of paid employment; rather, their way of life is determined by a government check each month. It is also clear that in spite of individual and collective actions attempting to improve the general quality of life, human emotion results in the creation and maintenance of a hierarchical structure where particular individuals have different experiences. An example occurred when a retired professional basketball player began to play tennis. At the end of the practice session, she did not realize she was responsible for maintaining the clay court. When handed a tool, her eyes seemed to convey uneasiness and a sense of entitlement. As one would expect, cultures of caring are difficult to obtain when certain individuals are perceived as more valuable than others.

In summary, acts of caring provide the quantifiable means to observe, record, and evaluate if human dignity is promoted or hindered. It appears that a global culture of caring does not exist and may be impossible to obtain because of the ambiguity associated with what behavior comprises acts of caring. In the future, the likelihood that acts of caring are defined and promoted is limited due to genetic and environmental variables that create significant variance in thoughts and actions. Therefore, despite historical efforts promoting broad societal change to improve the general quality of life, it is important to consider the outcome of emotion on human dignity.

OPPRESSION: THE NATURAL CONSEQUENCE OF EMOTION ON HUMAN DIGNITY

Various degrees of oppression result when emotion affects human dignity. In its traditional use, oppression means the exercise of tyranny by the ruling class (Grygier, 1954). Oppression denies members of certain groups the full range of human possibility that exists within a society and culture. From this standpoint, prejudice and racism are traditional constants aimed at reducing or diminishing the humanity of minority populations. As one would then expect, all the roles, places, and stereotypes forced upon the dominated group function to remove dignity by defining the person within frameworks that are less than or opposed to the status of full adulthood (Grygier, 1954). Throughout history, examples of overt oppression have been present all over the world. In India, for instance, thousands of couples each year use ultrasound to learn the sex of their unborn child. If the child is a girl, a three-thousand-year-old tradition celebrating sons and despising daughters may cause the child to be an abortion victim. For those girls who do survive, life is extremely difficult (Jerden, 1995). Similar religious beliefs across North Africa, the Middle East, and into Southern Asia keep women hidden and locked away, not subject to the influences of higher education, the modern world, or the Gospel (Jerden, 1995). In the United States, historical accounts of oppression describe how white males have received privileges as minorities have been systematically disadvantaged or excluded.

Exploitation, marginalization, powerlessness, cultural imperialism, and violence are the five faces of oppression (Young, 1990). Exploitation is the systematic process of labor in which the energies of the less fortunate are expended to maintain and augment the power, status, and wealth of the elite. Marginalization occurs when entire groups of individuals are expelled from useful participation in social life. In extreme cases, some adults are subjected to severe material deprivation and even extermination. Powerlessness arises when children and adults are conditioned to believe they have little control in their life to develop and exercise their skills. Cultural imperialism exists when members of the dominant group use their experiences and perceptions of reality to shape and develop cultural norms. Violence is the last face of oppression. Members of certain groups live with the knowledge and fear that they may experience random, unprovoked attacks that have no motive other than to damage humiliate or destroy (Young, 1990). Oppression in these five forms is a constant, invisible, binding restriction of existing economic, political, and cultural capital (Podgorecki, 1993).

More specifically, Regoli and Hewitt (1994) indicated that childhood oppression consists of individual, collective, or institutional actions. Individual oppression consists of adult behavior that directly produces negative consequences. Some babies for example are oppressed when their mothers use drugs or fathers smoke in their presence. Collective oppression involves patterns of behavior that allow youth to be oppressed by the larger society. It exists when citizens protest the high cost of public education and child health programs, object to emergency shelters being built in or around their neighborhoods, and allow stores, restaurants, health clubs, and housing complexes to prohibit children (Pogrebin, 1983). Finally, institutional oppression results within the context of social institutions, such as schools, families, and places of worship (Baldacci, 1991) . For example, currently one million school -aged children do not attend school. For those who do, some are enrolled in schools that are unheated or lack air conditioning, in buildings with leaking roofs, in classrooms without textbooks or lab equipment and qualified teachers (Kozol, 1991) . Outside the school, there are limited athletic fields and often no grounds at all, just trash-filled lots. Even in state-of-the- art schools, educators sometimes hinder the intellectual growth of children by having students listen to thousands of hours of lectures in order to complete tasks that require very little thinking (Schor, 1992). Childhood oppression provides an example of the vast and deep injustices some suffer because of unconscious assumptions and reactions of well-meaning people (Podgorecki, 1993).

Despite many emotion-driven societal movements, oppression has not disappeared but has changed to a more subtle form. Oppression today consists of a norm-referenced life perspective in which people determine their identity and value in comparison to others. This point of view frequently causes adults to feel trapped, searching for something such as a certain type of vocation or material possession to be perceived favorably. From a broader cultural standpoint, a norm-referenced life perspective heightens competition. Certain individuals or groups are perceived favorably or outstanding as others are thought of as limited or expendable. As this more subtle form of oppression unfolds and evolves, many adults continue to struggle with a lack of contentment, often feeling they have limited control in their life.

This norm-referenced form of oppression has become more apparent recently due to a number of variables. The most obvious is that the quality of life in industrialized countries has reached a level where most people have basic subsistence. As the standard of living increases, individuals have more time and energy to spend on tasks other than providing food and shelter for their family. In spite of these significant societal changes, human emotions still create an innate hunter and gatherer mentality among people. Today, financial portfolios, vacation homes, and other material possessions seem to have replaced the quest for water and game (deer, turkey, etc.). Another outcome of a higher standard of living is that many people have not experienced a lack of something. As a result, some appear to struggle determining the difference between what they need and want. This point is evident when you consider how many people feel that they should have an automobile, computer, cell phone, and designer clothing. Another related issue is associated with parents who want to make their child's life better than they experienced. It is perhaps possible that when adults provide youth more material possessions and opportunities, important life lessons may be missed, such as being responsible for your own actions and the value of work.

Changing attitudes toward employment and the availability of credit perpetuates this new form of oppression. For instance in the past, it was common to hear people say, "If I cannot pay for what I want, I will just have to live without it." This commonly held belief resulted in many adults being unwilling to accept assistance from someone else. This perspective on life changed in the United States when antipoverty government programs were implemented (Olasky, 1992). It became acceptable to receive welfare rather than performing menial tasks. Youth are now told that collecting garbage, digging ditches, or being a janitor was demeaning and that accepting government subsidy meant a person could at least keep their dignity (Olasky, 1992). Government programs as well caused many to evaluate their plight in life.

When individuals reflect upon and compare their experiences to others, it appears that painful emotions naturally surface, such as jealousy, fear, and helplessness. In response, many adults use the availability of credit to purchase material items to help them feel temporarily better.

The media also plays a significant role in shaping and maintaining a norm-referenced life perspective. Commercial advertising for instance conveys millions of messages each day that influence behavior. For example, some parents with limited resources purchase a pair of expensive Nike baby shoes. Obviously, their infant is unaware of the significance of the Nike shoes; however, the parents seem to want to convey a certain message to others around them. Network television characters and story lines also convey that personal success is associated with a certain body image, home, jewelry, and type of automobile. In addition, the advent of twenty-four-hour news stations has increased the media's role in shaping individual and collective perspectives. It appears that when information is repeated a certain number of times, children and adults begin to believe it as true when in actuality, it may not accurately reflect a diversity of viewpoints. Often, these messages are myths and misinformation such as associating happiness with money and material possessions. Adults who rely on the media to guide their thinking and daily behavior often are more likely to adopt a lifestyle that reflects a norm-referenced perspective.

As people experience this new form of oppression, three common responses occur. One is to withdraw and become socially invisible. In this situation, psychological and social pressures cause adults to feel humiliated, lacking confidence and hope (Moisi, 2009). The second is to engage in hyperconformist social interactions. Individuals become a part of a one-dimensional group congregating together and behaving in a similar fashion.

An example is when adults only associate with others who have similar beliefs. The third response is to go underground. Attempts are made to accomplish various tasks in secrecy from others while rejecting societal norms (Podgorecki, 1993). When using this approach, many spend their lifetime attempting to promote change even though traditions and personal attitudes make the task difficult if not impossible. Regardless of which coping strategy is used, all individuals to some degree experience episodic or constant states of oppression. As this emotion -based aspect of the human experience transpires, children and adults usually exhibit patterns of behavior that reflect a need for physical and psychological safety.

HUMAN RESPONSES TO OPPRESSION

Individuals search for a sense of belonging to offset the discomfort associated with feeling oppressed. In most instances, when adults identify with a certain individual or group, they seem to feel better. It is as if their identity is validated because others around them have similar beliefs and perspectives. This self-insulation preservation process begins when a young child demonstrates behavior like their mother, father, or other care provider. As teenagers, they typically adopt similar views as their parents while struggling to find their own particular sense of self. In the course of this complex life progression, a variety of coping strategies develop to buffer the feelings of oppression. Adults for example, who recently terminated a long relationship often communicate to those around them that they are not ready to become emotionally vulnerable. For some, it may take months or even years to feel they are prepared to invest the energy in a relationship. At a more concrete level, a common reaction to personal insecurity is to avoid experiences perceived as oppressive or dangerous. Many people for instance are unwilling to board an airplane, travel along certain roadways, or function without a weekly schedule. Another self-preservation strategy occurs for those who chose to use alcohol or other drugs to temporarily escape the pain experienced at a particular moment in time.

Labeling and categorizing is another common innate response to oppression. Children and adults gain a general sense of control and order when they are able to define and describe entities and experiences. Yet, when something does not fit neatly into a predetermined typology, it appears to create various levels of distress. An example is sometimes witnessed in an employment setting when a new person is hired. Initially, the employee is observed for a period of time by coworkers to determine if they are worthy of belonging to the existing group. If not, messages are sent to adapt to existing standards or explore other vocational opportunities. Classification also enables individuals to communicate about topics that are mutually understood. When people discuss common experiences, they seem to lessen their level of fear. This pattern of behavior may perhaps explain the growth and popularity of cell phones and other electronic communication devices. Another example to consider is how a person would feel if they entered a large department store that had items in no particular order. More than likely, feelings of confusion and disarray would cause them to leave the store. Labeling and categorizing people, places, and things allow individuals to feel in greater control of their life, thus lessening their sense of oppression.

A less obvious approach to offset oppression is to rationalize behavior. Rationalizations act as defense mechanisms to buffer or distort emotions. For example, when difficulties arise, many people state, "It's just the way it is, and I cannot do anything about it" or "I do not have any other choice." These assertions allow adults to move forward in their daily activities rather than dwelling on the emotions associated with a certain issue. In most cases, it appears that comparisons to others provide the foundation for rationalizations. For instance, it is common to hear the statement, "I can't do that. What will people think?" or "That's not how people do things here." In other situations, adults seem to feel better by comparing their plight in life to the graphic images of violence in Bosnia or starvation in Ethiopia. Many individuals perhaps might think but are hesitant to state, "At least I do not have to deal with what those poor people have too."

Despite the many innate characteristics and learned patterns of behavior used to offset oppression, people still struggle in life. For instance, increasing numbers of adults are experiencing depression and other challenging medical conditions. Others struggle with financial difficulties and personal relationships. As these current trends continue, countless numbers of individuals demonstrate limited understanding of how certain feelings result in choices that hinder their general quality of life. A daily example is how some respond to the concept of time. Many feel rushed and believe there are not enough hours in the day to meet the demands of living. This perspective may explain why most decisions are influenced more by emotion than intellect. When emotion plays a major role in judgment and decision making, individual and institutional change occurs at a very slow rate or does not happen at all. With this limited chance of societal and individual change, it too is highly unlikely that institutions will be able to create opportunities to offset the impact of emotion on human dignity.

MEASURING THE IMPACT OF EMOTION ON HUMAN DIGNITY

When measuring the effect of emotion on human dignity (oppression), it is vital to remember that efforts to quantify a theoretical construct are simply estimates that cannot be generalized across cultures, settings, genders, individuals, or any other significant variable. Therefore, the purpose of describing and computing levels of oppression is merely to promote dialogue that might be helpful. Six assumptions guide the attempt to quantify oppression:

1. Oppression is a natural, constant, of the human condition.
2. All cultures contain forms of oppression.
3. Oppression occurs in all environments.
4. No two individuals experience the same level of oppression.
5. Oppression impacts human identity development and psychological well-being.
6. The negative impact of oppression is determined based on the level of emotional vulnerability experienced at a particular point in time.

Bronfenbrenner's (1979) ecological theory provides the foundation to measure oppression. An ecological environment is thought of as a set of nested structures, each inside the next. At the innermost level is the immediate setting in which the individual functions. This can be a child's home or school. The next looks beyond single locations to the relation between them. How learning for example is impacted by neighborhood experiences. The third is yet further away and explores how a child's development is influenced by events occurring in locations in which they are not present. For instance, the work experiences of parents naturally impact the child in some way. Finally, within any culture, an organizational framework reflects common values that are distinctively different from others. Bronfenbrenner (1997) also suggested that individuals are embedded in a changing social, cultural, and economic environment, as well as being products of a life history of events, beliefs, and relationships.

With Bronfenbrenner's ideas in mind, it is important to accept when calculating oppression that individuals develop as a total integrated organism functioning within a vibrant evolving culture. Human development does not take place in single aspects taken out of context but rather is a series of complex dynamic processes that operate simultaneously in a nonlinear fashion. Individual development is therefore not an accumulation of outcomes but rather a process of restructuring subsystems and the whole structure within biological and social boundaries. More specifically, human beings are altered through an equilibrium model that contains an initial state of harmonious existence, emergence of some disruption, and time dependent movement toward the restoration of a state of harmony (Bronfrenbrenner, 1995). During this vigorous process, individuals lay the foundation of their psychological well-being while simultaneously establishing their identity. It might also be possible to suggest that the ongoing complexities associated with emotion, intellect, and their interaction promote or hinder personal wellness and human potential.

An example of this dynamic interactive process is someone attending a weeklong art class. Prior to the training, the individual reads and practices different activities obtaining a certain level of proficiency and confidence. While traveling to the training site, he experiences a variety of emotions and questions. Some of them include "What am I doing?" "What happens if I cannot pass the final test?" "What will my significant other think if I cannot get it?" Once arriving that evening at the hotel, a feeling of uncertainty and anticipation is present. On the first day of class, each participant is asked to create the same picture. When viewing their classmates work, many devalue their own performance regardless of the quality of their painting. As class requirements become steadily more difficult, a variety of emotions related to self-doubt intensify. In response, some cry, swear, and threaten to leave while others criticize the method of instruction. As the week progresses, a few participants are able to advance in their skill level while others remain in a state of psychological disharmony. For those who are able to gain the confidence to continue, further learning occurs, while those in emotional upheaval remain in a state of limited growth.

Before attempting to analyze and quantify oppression in the aforementioned example, it might be helpful to review some of the complexities of human emotion. Human genetics provides the foundation for the specific feelings associated with each life experience. Initially, young children process stimuli in ways that allow them to feel safe while attempting to make sense of the world around them. As they become older, their innate endowment coupled with life experiences shape their identity and the level of safety and security needed to function. In most situations, however, when children and adults experience feelings of discomfort, the autonomic nervous system to some degree shifts from the parasympathetic (normal functioning) to sympathetic system (fight or flight mechanism). Some people remain in this primitive survival physiological state for long periods while others use a variety of coping mechanisms to gain a sense of relief and comfort. In spite of this innate response, the amount of time spent in psychological disequilibrium often determines individual energy levels. It too appears that when adults respond negatively to discomfort rather than perceiving it as an opportunity to learn, they lose a certain degree of energy needed to promote their own growth.

Now that we have briefly reviewed the complexities of emotion, it is time to return to the art class. Self-reports and video observations were used to determine the level of oppression experienced during the weeklong training session. Two one-hour interviews were conducted at the end of the week and one month after training. A third two-hour interview occurred six weeks after training. Interviews were audio-taped and transcribed. During the initial interview, the participant was asked general questions such as "How did you feel at the beginning, middle, and end of training?" After five questions, three seven-minute video segments were shown. The researcher asked a variety of descriptive and probing questions based on the activities observed. During the second hour of the third interview, the researcher discussed the concept of oppression. The subject along with the researcher then used a cardinal scale beginning with the number one (low) and ending with ten (extreme) to calculate the level of oppression experienced. After a lengthy discussion, the participant concluded that her innate characteristics and life experiences resulted in a score of four on the oppression scale. Despite the structured research protocol, the quantifying of oppression regardless of methodology used will not meet the rigor of scientific inquiry. For example, the variability in genetic traits, differences in life experiences, and their interaction is impossible to measure. Additionally, the relationship between the researcher and subject, a lack of baseline data, sample size, and content of interview questions limit the accuracy and generalizability of the oppression score. Thus, the quantification of oppression is merely an attempt to stimulate discussion of how individuals interact with each other and the role emotion plays on human dignity.

CHAPTER SUMMARY

Human emotion is the reason why individuals struggle promoting the dignity of each other. Emotion is the energy that drives, organizes, amplifies and attenuates cognitive activity within the socially influenced value-appraising process of the brain (Siegel, 1999). Measuring and analyzing acts of caring is one possible way to determine the extent in which emotion impacts human dignity. Caring is a loving feeling exhibiting concern and empathy for others (Merriam -Webster Online Dictionary, 2009). Acts of caring could further be described along a continuum beginning with a level of self-centeredness unaware of those around you, ending, with the giving of ones life to preserve another. It was also suggested that innate emotional differences among people may explain why a culture of caring does not exist and may be impossible to obtain.

Oppression is the natural consequence of emotions impact on human dignity. In its traditional usage, oppression means the exercise of tyranny by a ruling class denying members of certain groups the full range of human possibility that exists within a society and culture (Grygier, 1954). All the roles, places, and stereotypes function to remove dignity by defining the person within frameworks that are less than or opposed to the status of full adulthood. In more recent times, emotion-driven collective and individual actions have resulted in greater opportunities to vote, increased participation in religious activities, and access to private and public institutions. Oppression however, has not disappeared, but has evolved into a more subtle form consisting of a norm referenced life perspective. Children and adults are now conditioned to determine their identity and worth in comparison to others. As a result, some seem trapped in a constant whirlwind searching for a certain type of vocation or material possession. From a broader cultural standpoint, a norm referenced life perspective heightens competition as certain individuals and groups such as, doctors and service members are thought of as local community heroes, while criminals and those unemployed are perceived as limited, static, and expendable. As this new form of oppression continues to evolve and unfold, many struggle with a lack of personal safety, believing they have limited control in life. To offset these difficult feelings, individuals sometimes develop a variety of coping strategies that hinder human dignity.

Bronfenbrenner (1979, 1995 & 1997) ecological theory provided the foundation to measure oppression. An ecological environment is thought of as a set of nested structures, each inside the next. At the innermost level is the immediate setting, the next looks beyond single locations to the relation between them. The third level is yet further away; it explores how individual growth and development is impacted by events occurring in locations in which they are not present. Finally, within any culture an organizational framework reflects common values that are distinctively different from others (Bronfenbrenner, 1979). It was also suggested that human development does not take place in single aspects taken out of context, but rather as a series of complex dynamic processes that operate simultaneously in a nonlinear fashion. Individual skill development is therefore not an accumulation of outcomes but rather a process of restructuring subsystems and the whole structure within biological and social boundaries. More specifically, human beings are altered through an equilibrium model that contains an initial state of harmonious existence, emergence of some disruption, and time dependent movement toward the restoration of a state of harmony (Bronfenbrenner, 1995). To illuminate this dynamic interactive process, an art class example was presented.

Now that we have explored emotion and human dignity, it is time to consider another abstract idea: emotions impact on human talent. That topic will be explored in the upcoming chapter.

EMOTION AND HUMAN TALENT

The quality of one's life is often determined by human ability coupled with environmental resources. Naturally, inhabitants of certain locations are more fortunate than others due to genetics along with social and political variables that identify, nurture, and leverage human capital. Human capital is therefore not only a bank account, a thousand shares of General Electric stock, but also competencies, knowledge, and personality attributes embodied in the ability to perform labor of economic value (Becker, 1993; Sullivan and Sheffrin, 2003). Specific human capital as well refers to skills or knowledge that is useful only to a single employer or industry, whereas general human capital (such as literacy) is useful to all employers. Education is thought to be one of the most important investments in human capital (Becker, 1993) . For example, over the past fifty years in the United States, those with a college degree earned approximately 45 percent more than high school graduates. In the 1960s, this number rose to almost 60 percent and in recent accounts has reached a high of 75 percent in 1997 (National Center for Education Statistics, 2004).

Despite these extensive economic studies and theories involving human capital, collective and individual talents go beyond those which might be easily identified or measured. With this thought in mind, this chapter explores how the complexities of emotion may impact human talent. An enhanced understanding of this complex dynamic might result in an increased probability of individual and collective change. To begin the study, emotion is defined and discussed within the context of daily activities.

EMOTION

Emotion is defined as a complex state of feeling that results in physiological and psychological changes that impact thoughts and actions. From a broad cultural perspective, human emotion historically has created and maintained a social order where certain individuals or groups obtain higher status than others. As this hierarchical structure unfolds, a general sense of competition permeates throughout society. For example, it appears that individuals who have innate abilities or are capable of performing vocations such as medicine and law are perceived as more valuable than others. What is further evident is how this idea is reinforced by the levels of education required for certain vocations. Another obvious delineation is found in the clothes people wear. Suits and ties are expected of lawyers, doctors have white coats, and educators' attires are casual. In other instances, if adults have their name stitched on their work clothes, some members of society perceive and treat them as though they have limited abilities. Another more specific example of social status is found with entertainers who have children who have autism spectrum disorders. It seems that their physical appearance coupled with their latest movie or television show allows them to have a forum to share their experiences when others do not.

The emotions associated with the id, ego, and superego

shape personality development (Freud, 1938). The id, the largest portion of the mind, is inherited and present at birth. It is the source of basic biological needs and desires. The ego is the conscious, rational part of personality that emerges in infancy to ensure that the id's desires are satisfied in accord with reality. The superego, or seat of conscience, contains the values of society. Once the superego is formed, the emotions associated with ego redirect impulses so they are exhibited on appropriate objects at acceptable times and places (Freud, 1938). A natural consequence of this uniquely human balancing of id, ego, and superego is learning. Learning is defined as acquiring, comprehending, and using information to solve real-life problems (Berk, 1998). The amount of information known on a subject is typically referred to as depth of understanding. It seems relatively clear that a person's level of content knowledge is determined subjectively, beginning with awareness and continuing indefinitely. A simplistic example is someone learning to play the piano; they begin with basic notes and corresponding keys, simple scales and songs increasing in complexity. With time and extensive practice, the musician will transition from novice to skilled performer.

Human emotions impact talent development. An example is sometimes noticed when observing two individuals in a conversation. When one person creates a sense of uneasiness for the other, the listener to some degree does not hear what is being said because their basic survival instinct is activated to protect themselves. Further observation reveals that subtle nonverbal messages are usually conveyed to change the topic or end the conversation, thus preventing participants from gaining information that could enhance their depth of understanding. In contrast, if a certain level of emotional intimacy exists between the individuals, further dialogue may result in greater levels of topic knowledge. Another variable associated with the development of talent is the frequency and intensity of previous emotional violations. When a person has had difficulties in the past, they are hesitant to take risks in the future. For instance, if someone was treated as if they were academically incapable, they would be more likely not to attempt challenging mathematical problems. In extreme cases such as when a student is told by their teacher they are dumb and stupid, they may become emotionally paralyzed, unable to progress in their skill development. Temporary fluctuations in emotions as well seem to influence a person's ability to obtain and retain information at a given point in time.

More specifically, feelings of fear, shame, and guilt have the greatest impact on human talent. Emotions such as these have the potential to alter every aspect of existence ranging from life expectancy, human interactions, environmental erosion, and the gross domestic product. It appears that when an individual spends a large amount of time in a state of emotional turmoil, they do not cultivate their own talent but rather respond in ways that promote a sense of safety. For instance, adults sometimes deprive themselves of certain experiences such as riding an airplane or venturing too far from their families because they are afraid. What is also evident is that when emotional barriers are challenged, a sensation of discomfort naturally results in attempts to escape the situation. An example of this pattern of behavior is often noticed after an individual has recently been divorced. When meeting someone new, regardless of their initial physical attraction, they communicate subtle messages that act to push the other person away. In some instances, it may take months or even years for them to participate in a new relationship.

The perception of time is also impacted by emotion. Many adults feel that there are simply not enough hours in a day to get everything finished. This sentiment is reflected in statements such as "I just cannot get things done no matter how hard I try" or "I do not even have enough time to catch my breath some days." This general sense that life is a whirlwind causes some individuals to not identify and promote their innate talent or the skill sets of others. Difficulties with the concept of time may also explain why individual and institutional change occurs at a very slow rate or does not happen at all. For instance, how can someone study the complexity of an issue when feeling they barely have time to meet their own basic needs? The answer to this important question may explain why academic activities in public schools today are not much different than in the 1940s. Children still sit in desks in straight rows and listen to lectures in spite of research indicating other more effective teaching strategies.

Many other emotion-based behaviors affect human talent. For instance, in the United States, nearly one in five Cornell and Princeton University students surveyed stated they have purposefully injured themselves by cutting, burning, or other methods to help relieve stress or make deep emotional wounds more visible (Tanner, 2006). Sarah Roney, a University of Illinois student, acknowledged, "Self-abuse was part of waking up, getting dressed, the last look in the mirror, and then the cut on the wrist. I couldn't have a perfect day without it." Other outward signs of emotional discomfort might possibly range from rocking in a chair, continually tapping a foot on the floor, and tattooing or piercing a body part. Tremendous variation and changes in individual behavior patterns also cause some to wonder what is happening as they cannot make sense of the actions around them. These intense feelings sometimes distort reality and typically create a cyclical response pattern in which a person has an experience, an emotion is generated, and if discomfort is present, a response is exhibited to lessen the uneasiness. An example is sometimes noticed in a work environment. When someone is hired, an instinctive sense of discomfort is present as they speculate how their employer perceives them. These unsettling feelings may result in oversensitivity and less productivity. In other instances, if the new employee has previous negative work experiences, they will attempt to gain comfort by talking to a coworker or participating in other activities. If they continue this pattern of behavior in response to difficult situations, they may not cultivate their talent but rather participate in activities that meet their most basic emotional needs.

A continuum beginning with soft-open and ending with hard-closed might be helpful to think further about the role of emotion on human talent. Points along the scale indicate the level of risk someone is willing to take to cultivate their talent. At birth, infants begin at soft, and as life experiences unfold, the frequency and intensity of certain emotions determine the degree in which someone becomes emotionally hardened. What seems evident from this conceptualization is that despite innate resiliency, periods of limited need fulfillment cause a number of children and adults to land closer to hard-closed rather than soft-open. As this occurs, survival instincts rather than intellectual enlightenment seem to guide the level of risk someone is willing to experience. It might also be possible to suggest that the number of adults emotionally hardened at any particular point in time determines the probability in which innate talent is identified and nurtured.

EMOTION AND TALENT: HUMAN GROWTH AND DEVELOPMENT

Human growth and development areas will be used to frame the discussion on how emotion impacts human talent. Readers should not infer that the author believes that it is possible to simplify individual growth and development into categories; however, it is one way to think about a complex evolving dynamic. Areas considered include physical, cognitive, social, and moral.

PHYSICAL

Physical development impacts innate talent. Berk (1998) indicated that during the first two years of life, an individual grows more rapidly than any time after birth. At the age of five months, birth weight has doubled, and at the end of the first year, an infant is approximately 50 percent longer. Adequate nutrition is critical at this time of life as 25 percent of calories are used to keep rapidly developing organs functioning properly. Also, at birth, the brain is closer to its adult size than any other physical structure. The human brain has one hundred to two hundred billion neurons that release chemicals that cross the synapse, sending messages to one another. As neurons form connections, stimulation becomes important in their survival. Neurons that are stimulated by input from the surrounding environment continue to establish new synapses. Those that are seldom aroused soon die off (Berk, 1998).

The manner in which emotion impacts physical growth is perhaps captured in the theory of failure to thrive. Failure to thrive is defined as decelerated or arrested physical growth associated with poor developmental and emotional functioning (Kessler and Dawson, 1999). This phenomenon usually occurs in children younger than two years old who have no known medical condition. Infants experiencing failure to thrive have bodies that look malnourished and are withdrawn and apathetic. Another related emotion-based issue is associated with the availability and digestion of food. It seems that even if a variety of food is present and consumed, children and adults may be malnourished because certain nutrients might be lost while in emotional discomfort. For some people, eating is also used as a means to cope with difficult experiences. As this occurs, individuals may experience a variety of physical ailments associated with the overindulgence or underindulgence of food.

The amount of stress someone experiences also impacts physical health. For some, genetic endowment coupled with the indoctrination process results in increased physical, mental, or emotional tension. As this occurs, an individual's immune system may be comprised, increasing the risk for various viruses, cardiovascular disease, certain forms of cancer, and a variety of autoimmune disorders (Berk, 1998). Stress also creates or exacerbates difficulties in sleeping. As people age, they naturally have more trouble falling asleep, staying asleep, and sleeping deeply due to changes in brain structure and higher levels of stress hormones in the bloodstream (Whitbourne, 1996). Without enough rest, children and adults are likely to become more self-centered in order to offset discomfort and pain. An example of this may have occurred when a number of individuals phoned a friend after hip surgery. The conversation, in some cases, quickly transitioned from the needs of the individual to the caller. Was the caller really concerned or was it simply an opportunity to lessen their own discomfort? It is relatively clear that emotion in some situations may not allow individuals to feel physically well enough to identity and nurture human talent.

COGNITIVE

Cognitive ability is a major component of human talent. Piaget (1930) suggested that cognitive development takes place in stages characterized by qualitatively distinct ways of thinking. In the sensorimotor stage (birth to two years), infants use their senses to explore the world. They often invent ways to locate desired objects or obtain attention from those around them. These patterns of behavior evolve into the symbolic but illogical thinking of the preschooler in the preoperational stage (two to seven years). Language skills are beginning to develop during this time period. Then cognition is transformed into the more organized reasoning of the school- age child in the concrete operational stage (seven to eleven years). Children are able to arrange objects into categories based on some identifying feature. Finally, in the formal operation stage (eleven years and beyond), thought becomes more abstract as individuals have the ability to identify options to solve complex problems (Piaget, 1930). Piaget also used the term *schemes* to represent the psychological structures needed for cognitive development. At the beginning of life, schemes represent motor action patterns such as the taking apart, banging, and the dropping of plastic cups. Most infants usually discover that as the cups drop, they influence one another, and predictable outcomes will result. As children then become older, adaptation and organization account for changes in thinking. Adaptation involves direct interaction with the environment. It consists of two complementary actions: assimilation and accommodation (Piaget, 1952). During assimilation, current schemes are used to interpret the external world. In accommodation, individuals create new schemes or adjust old ones after determining that their current way of thinking cannot explain recent experiences. Schemes change as well through a second internal process called organization. Once a child forms new schemes, they rearrange and link them with others to create a strongly interconnected cognitive system (Piaget, 1952).

Many aspects of Piaget's cognitive developmental theory are impacted by emotion. The most obvious is the perception of stimuli. If a pattern of lack of emotional support is present, an individual may distort information and demonstrate actions that hinder cognitive growth. An example sometimes occurs when a child or adult has an intense need for a sense of belonging. They often spend an inordinate amount of time and energy worrying about how others perceive them rather than attempting to expand their cognitive ability. What is further noticed is that once feelings of belonging are met, individuals sometimes become psychological comfortable and rigid in their thinking. Memory skills essential for intellectual growth are also impacted by emotion. It appears that information entering short - and long-term memory is determined based on the depth or intensity of emotion associated with certain experiences. For example, if a child or adult feels they have been harmed in someway by their parents, friends, teachers, or employer, they are more likely to recall the exact events. In contrast, if they have a pleasant experience with someone, they are less likely to remember what was specifically stated. Another example of emotions role in cognitive development is noticed when individuals interpret stimuli differently in a shared experience. Variations in what is heard, understood, and remembered may reflect emotional responses to voice tone, pitch, rate, color, texture, and nonverbal messages.

The emotions associated with fear appear to have the greatest impact on cognitive development. If the perception of danger is present, basic survival instincts may lessen someone's ability to gain information from the environment. These thoughts might range from physical attacks to general and specific feelings of discomfort related to certain individuals and activities. An example is sometimes noticed when an elementary school student is required to participate in cooperative group activities. He may be unwilling to take risks in his learning if other students have laughed at him in the past or the teacher has inadvertently made him feel as though he is incapable. Fear might further explain why some adults have to directly experience something before it enters their consciousness and understanding. It may also be possible to suggest that the extent in which information is gained, comprehended, and stored in memory is determined by the level of fear existing at a particular point in time.

Fear, along with other emotions, may explain why adults sometimes exhibit adolescent-type behavior. It seems that when individuals experience frequent and intense periods of emotional discomfort, they become stagnant in their level of knowledge and perhaps paralyzed in their ability to develop cognitive skills. An example sometimes occurs when a loved one in the military is in harm's way. In spite of his strong desire to learn while attending college, worry may hinder his capacity to obtain a level of concentration needed to acquire, comprehend, and retain new information. What is also noticed is that adults naturally congregate with others who exhibit similar fear-based actions. As this unfolds, an ongoing cycle of emotional upheaval lessens the probability in which cognitive skills are identified and developed. Individuals clearly must move beyond emotion-based responses in order to nurture and maximize their innate cognitive ability.

SOCIAL

Innate talent is sometimes reflected in social capital. Social capital refers to the ability to use memberships and relationship connections in groups and networks to gain benefit (Soebel, 2002) . As citizens participate in neighborhood associations, unions, and sports clubs, increases in stocks of social capital are available in the future. Social capital is also thought to be comprised of trust and solidarity, collective action and cooperation, social cohesion and inclusion, and information (Halpren, 2004). Woolcock (2001) identified three common types of social capital. Bonding social capital denotes connections between adults in similar situations, such as immediate family, close friends, and neighbors. Bridging social capital consists of more distant ties of like persons, such as acquaintances and coworkers. Linking social capital reaches out to dissimilar individuals in certain situations to leverage a broader range of resources. Regardless of the type of social capital, each is dependent on communication skills to foster relationships between individuals and groups (Woolcock, 2001).

For communication to occur there must be shared physical or digital space, and a common language channel existing between individuals. Initially, the sender conveys an idea, perception, or feeling nonverbally and in spoken or written language. The receiver then interprets the message based on their personal reality. Once meaning has been assigned, a corresponding nonverbal and verbal response is usually emitted. This ongoing sequence of events typically continues until a participant voluntarily stops talking, walks away, or does not respond to electronic transmissions of information. Successful communication is then considered to have taken place if the perceived message approximates the intent of the sender. In spite of this simplistic linear description, communication is not an absolute finite process. More specifically, communication is often vague and misleading. For instance, if the sender says a word such as *closure*, she has a certain meaning attached to it that might not reflect how others perceive the term. A possible reason as to why this occurs is that the emotions associated with past experiences filter and shape how messages are conveyed, understood, and corresponding actions are exhibited. It is also evident within the communication process that when adults are in a positive mood, they are more sensitive to changes in voice tone and subtle nonverbal messages. In contrast, if someone is experiencing fear and doubt, they may be unable to look beyond there own immediate needs to gather and interpret information. This lack of sensitivity toward others sometimes causes them to have difficulties assessing and adapting to the communication demands of their environment.

The emotions conveyed through various communication mediums impact social capital. A sense of closeness or uneasiness naturally develops between individuals as they share experiences. It appears that a person's frame of reference at a particular point in time influences the extent and quality of interaction. For instance, if someone is physically tired or is reminded of an individual they dislike, they may misconstrue the message and end the dialogue. However, the discussion will usually continue if thoughts are expressed similar to the listeners' ideas. Emotions as well impact the ability to understand verbal and nonverbal messages. When individuals encounter stimuli creating discomfort, they sometimes misinterpret information while simultaneously demonstrating a variety of coping behaviors. As these actions develop and evolve, an approach -avoidance dichotomy shapes the type, frequency, and content of future experiences. An example of this is how adults react to youth who have multiple body piercing. In some instances, they become intellectually paralyzed with the question, "Why would anyone do that to their body?" not taking the opportunity to interact with someone that could positively alter their life. This pattern of avoidance and lack of understanding may be traced to the instinctive self-preservation fear response.

In order to gain social capital, it appears that adults need to accept that aspects of life naturally unfold. Certain outcomes regardless of specific actions happen for no apparent reason. The most obvious example is weather phenomenon. As a tornado touches the ground, little explanation can be provided why certain areas are devastated while others are not. If and when individuals realize and accept that they have limited control in life, they seem to become empowered, able to identify and reflect upon past experiences that have shaped their identity. This personal enlightenment enhances their ability to appreciate and sympathize with others in different circumstances other than their own. Another frequent outcome of this increased self-awareness is that they gain creditability in the eyes of those around them. In contrast, if emotion results in judging and labeling others, they may lose opportunities to acquire the social capital needed to improve their general quality of life.

MORAL

Morality is another human growth and development area impacted by emotion. Morality refers to the principles of right and wrong conduct (Webster, 1993). Its development is thought to occur in six unique stages (Kohlberg, 1969).

At stage one, punishment and obedience, children find it difficult to consider two points of view. As a result, they ignore the intentions of others while focusing on their fear of authority and avoidance of punishment.

During stage two, instrumental purpose, children become aware that others can have different perspectives. Right actions are those that satisfy personal needs.

Individuals in stage three, "good boy-good girl," seek to maintain the affection and approval of friends and relatives. Often, they attempt to be trustworthy, loyal, respectful, helpful, and nice in order to be perceived as a good person.

In stage four, the social-order-maintaining orientation, moral choice no longer depends on close ties to others. Instead, rules must be enforced in the same fashion for everyone, and each member of society has a personal duty to uphold them.

For those in stage five, social contract, laws, and rules are regarded as flexible instruments for furthering human purposes. Each person is a free and willing participant in the system because it brings about more good than if it did not exist.

The last and highest stage, the universal ethical principle, defines right action as that which is valid for all humanity, regardless of law and social agreement. These abstract values include consideration of the claims of all human beings and respect for the worth and dignity of each person (Kohlberg, 1969).

Moral development is highly dependent on the ability to reason (Kochanska, Casey and Fukumoto, 1995). This aptitude evolves as individuals experience a variety of people and events in their environment. It appears that when adults reach a certain level of cognitive ability and emotional self-awareness, they rely less on external agents such as law enforcement to gain a sense of order. In contrast, adults who have limited intellect seem to experience some level of confusion regarding what is and is not acceptable behavior. This ambiguity often results in the creation and reliance on policies and procedures to guide actions. One such example occurred in a local hospital. The administrator was told that employees in the kitchen were driving their cars to the back of the building and stealing food. Once investigated and found to be true, someone suggested that a policy should be written to make sure that everyone knew that it was inappropriate to steal. Granted, this is an extreme example; nonetheless, it reflects how emotion may impact the ability to reason logically.

To some degree, physiological responses to stimuli affect moral reasoning. As adrenaline is produced in reaction to the perception of possible harm, individuals have an increased likelihood of misinterpreting information due to their immediate need for safety. An example is noticed when individuals verbalize certain behavior as appropriate; yet, their actions contradict their words. For instance, many adults verbalize their love for children but are unwilling to pay additional taxes to promote their learning. Do they really care about their welfare, or is it simply a conditioned response? Other examples of how emotion impacts moral decision making might be witnessed in the increasing number of adults who experience road rage, detrimental spending and eating habits, and use of illegal substances.

A number of outcomes result when emotion impacts moral development. The most noticeable is that societies divide themselves into smaller self-defined groups, distinct and separate from the larger population. Certain individuals or groups naturally gravitate toward others who share common characteristics and similar beliefs. This sense of belonging and camaraderie provides the foundation for psychological health; however, this behavior may result in emotional stagnation, self-oppression, and divisiveness within and between various groups of people. This is evident when you consider the United States political system. Republicans and Democrats compete tirelessly against each other while attempting to solve issues of concern. As this ongoing struggle unfolds, many adults seem to become more insensitive and judgmental. The mind-set that "I am right, and you are wrong" triggers emotion and exacerbates the confusion over what is and is not morally correct behavior. In response, many demonstrate behavior indicating they feel as though they have little control in their life and that they have been victimized by something. To offset these intense feelings, most actions, regardless of the individual, are to some degree self-serving.

After considering how emotions might impact physical, cognitive, social, and moral development, one can conclude that how a person feels at a certain point in time impacts the level and trajectory in which skills develop. Innately, variations of basic survival instincts act as the foundation for the possibility of talent development. Emotion, more so than intellect, seems to then determine the level of energy children and adults have to acquire information from their environment. As this aspect of the human experience unfolds, someone's talent does not develop in isolation or within a vacuum but rather is shaped by experiences within families, schools, and information from the media.

CONTEXTUAL VARIABLES: SHAPING EMOTIONS THAT PROMOTE OR HINDER HUMAN TALENT

A person's genetic endowment provides the foundation for talent. Moreover, skills are more likely to develop in certain individuals rather than others. For some, creativity and artistic aptitude is evident while others posses the ability to manipulate tools to perform desired tasks. An important question to consider in this reality of life is why certain innate talents remain dormant while others are activated and cultivated. As one would perhaps expect, an individual's family plays a significant role in identifying and shaping innate talent. Berk (1998) implied that parenting styles may nurture or oppress ability. For example, authoritative parents provide rules and discuss reasons for them. As children demonstrate increased ability to self-regulate their behavior, they are given more responsibility. Children who live in these types of families tend to be self-motivated, assertive, and able to work productively with others. Authoritarian parents, however, establish rules for their children's behavior and expect them to be blindly obeyed. Explanations for why a particular rule is necessary are almost never given. This parenting approach promotes a lack of warmth and fosters resentment between the child and parent. In contrast, permissive parents provide little guidance and allow their children to decide almost everything, such as what to eat, wear, and when to go to bed (Baumrind, 1991). Children living in this situation are markedly less assertive and usually lack fundamental cognitive skills. Similarly, rejecting -neglecting parents do not make demands on their children or respond to their emotional needs. Adults are not only nonsupportive of their children's goals and activities, they may actively reject or neglect their parenting responsibilities (Baumrind, 1991).

The attitudes, skills, and experiences of family members provide a model for talent development. If an older brother for instance is a star athlete, resources are more likely to be allocated to provide similar opportunities. As this occurs, a child may have limited chance of uncovering nonathletic abilities. Additionally, the frequency and type of interaction between a child and their extended family may nurture or oppress talent. For example, if a highly educated uncle lives thousands of miles away, he will have few opportunities to teach his nieces and nephews certain skills. To think more about how families impact talent development, an emotion-based continuum beginning with calmness ending with upheaval might be helpful. From this conceptualization, one could possibly suggest that if a child's parents spend the majority of time closer to upheaval than calmness, they are less likely able to identify and nurture their own talent and that of their child. Family income also impacts talent development. The greater the amount of resources available, the more likely a child will be exposed to opportunities. An example would be two children who have a proclivity for science. If one experiences a science camp and not the other, the skills of the unexposed youth are more prone to remain dormant and unidentified. Money is clearly not everything; however, it does create a context for the possibility of talent development.

SCHOOLS

The educational experiences of youth impact talent development. Two philosophical approaches have historically guided American schools: traditional and open (Skinner and Belmont, 1993). In a traditional classroom, children are relatively passive in the learning process as the teacher does most of the talking while students spend time at their desks listening, responding when called on, and completing assigned tasks. Student progress is determined by how well they perform on a uniform set of standards for their grade. In contrast, teachers in open classrooms assume a flexible authority role, sharing decision making with students as they work at their own pace to create knowledge. Student performance is evaluated in relation to prior development (Skinner and Belmont, 1993). Currently, in the United States, The No Child Left Behind Act of 2001 is promoting a more traditional approach. This act requires students to achieve grade level proficiency on standardized reading and mathematics examinations. If they do not meet adequate yearly progress, school districts face sanctions ranging from writing improvement plans to the state department of education determining if principals should maintain employment, teachers should receive pay raises, and if schools should stay open. This emphasis on standardized test results cause students regardless of age to often work silently and alone on seatwork that is clearly driven by skills measured on standardized achievement tests. In many instances, children now perceive school as simply a series of tasks that need completion to advance to the next grade level; limited academic growth occurs when the joy of learning is absent.

Changes in school experiences have resulted from another educational trend: the inclusion movement. In inclusive schools and classrooms, emphasis is placed on building communities with everyone's gifts and talents recognized and utilized to the fullest extent possible (Turnbull, Turnbull, Shank, and Leal, 2010). Each individual is thought of as a worthwhile member of the group who has a role to play in supporting others to foster self-esteem, pride in peer accomplishment, mutual respect, and a sense of belonging. Two consequences seem to result from this relatively new philosophical idea: class sizes are larger and vast learning differences exist between students. To offset these changes, special and regular education professionals work in collaboration to design learning opportunities that are sensitive to all learners (Hardman, Drew, and Egan, 2006). This change in professional roles and the constantly evolving learning environment appear to create a great deal of anxiety and confusion among students and education professionals.

As the standardization and acceptance of diversity movements have been implemented, little emphasis has been placed on the identification and cultivation of talent. Rather, accountability and equality guide education decision making. A natural outcome of this perspective is that the roles of educators have changed. In many school systems, teachers are made to feel as though they cannot veer from the scripted curriculum. If they do so, they may be in danger of receiving a poor evaluation and eventually lose their job. Teachers, as well, are expected to cover vast amounts of information in a relatively short period of time. This quantity rather than quality mind-set has resulted in many students struggling with their depth of content knowledge. Ultimately, how educators respond to these current trends will determine the extent in which they cultivate and nurture their own talent and that of their students. Another education reality is that in some school districts, students have limited exposure to content areas that are not measured on standardized tests. This narrow approach to curriculum and learning may oppress rather than nurture talent development.

The general structure and culture of the education system also creates obstacles for talent development. For instance, the level of compensation provided teachers results in many bright individuals choosing other disciplines. For those who do teach, the work environment seems to permeate fear rather than joy, as educators are asked to do more with less. It also appears that the focus of education is national security (see *Nation at Risk*, 1983) rather than individual empowerment. A common consequence of this type of thinking is that limited thought and energy seems invested in creating curriculum opportunities that are sensitive to advanced or nontraditional learners. In the end, most individuals in the field of education are well intended; yet, significant amounts of human talent may remain dormant or receive little cultivation due to lack of stimulation and opportunity.

MEDIA

The media plays a significant role in shaping human talent. Media can be defined as a means of communication, such as radio, television, newspaper, and Internet (Webster, 1993). A variety of information is now available such as international, national, and local news, music videos, and television shows portraying various story lines. Elkind (2001) indicated that most children consume approximately forty hours of media a week and twenty thousand commercials a year. He also suggested a number of reasons why children and adults are spending increasing amounts of time interacting with media. One, some parents are concerned about the safety of their neighborhood and do not allow their children to play unsupervised. The need to occupy their children's time results in increased television viewing. Another less obvious explanation is that many enjoy the physiological stimulation gained through animation and various levels of sound. Third, students now have the opportunity to gain access to formal education through the Internet. These programs allow individuals to learn at any time of the day and do not require travel to a specific educational setting (Elkind, 2001).

Unintended outcomes result from increased media interactions. The most obvious is that children and adults struggle differentiating between what is fantasy and what is real. For some, repeated replay of school shootings and child abductions desensitize while simultaneously creating a culture of fear (Glassner, 1999). Another outcome is a general state of confusion and disillusion; entertainers push the envelope, to gain a reaction that promotes themselves or a certain television show. An example of this occurred when a costume malfunctioned during a Super Bowl halftime show. The events were talked about for weeks with a variety of political and social leaders participating in discussions related to parenting, advertising, and corporate and individual responsibility. Increased use of media also contributes to physical ailments. Many children and adults struggle obtaining optimal health due to the number of hours spent passively watching television or searching the Internet.

The characteristics of those portrayed in the media impact talent development. Viewers are now conditioned to believe that certain levels of status and prestige are associated with being an athlete, entertainer, doctor, fireman, or teacher. These overt and subtle messages coupled with the innate human need to be perceived favorably results in many individuals expending energy on tasks that may not be possible. Evidence of this is sometimes noticed when interacting with adolescent boys. When you ask them what they want to be when they grow up, in many instances, they would say, "I want to be a football or basketball player." Under any circumstance, would a young person state, "I want to be a janitor when I get older"? Media messages also impact adults. A person's identity and level of success is often shaped and evaluated based on some standard that is disseminated through the media. For many, a certain car or size of home is thought to be an indicator that someone is doing well in life. Statements such as, "He must be doing all right, he is driving a Lexus isn't he?" illuminate this common way of thinking.

Three other common outcomes result from the media's impact on talent development. The most obvious is that children and adults are conditioned to believe that certain endeavors are more important than others. This way of thinking creates a hierarchal social structure that promotes division rather than cohesion among people. A possible consequence of this is that innate talent may be more likely to remain dormant when children and adults do not interact or gain intellectual stimulation from those who are different from them. Second, the media promotes passive rather than active thinking. In most instances, television programs do not promote thought but rather allow individuals to divert their attention away from the activities of daily living. Lastly, and perhaps most importantly, the media conveys sounds and images at a rate that promotes limited processing of information. This might explain why if someone has not directly experienced something, they have limited ability to recall or understand certain events. A recent example might be the series of earthquakes experienced in Japan. Few individuals will remember the devastation if they themselves have not had that experience. The rate of verbal and visual input may also trigger physiological-based responses associated with fear and anxiety. It appears that the media in many instances acts as an oppressor rather than cultivator of talent.

When summarizing the role of contextual variables on innate talent, one must accept that a person's genetic endowment provides the foundation for talent. Certain skills are more likely to develop in particular individuals rather than others. Innate aptitude is of course impacted to some degree by family, school, and media. This aspect of the human condition begins with the type and frequency of interaction occurring between an infant and their care provider. As children become older, parenting styles along with information gained while at school or through the media act in some way to nurture or hinder native talent. It might also be possible to conclude that the probability in which innate talent surfaces and is cultivated depends on the emotional well-being of those involved in the daily activities of living.

TALENT AND THE DAILY ACTIVITIES OF LIFE

The ability to identify, develop, and use one's talent is often determined by how individuals feel prior to or after responding to certain environmental stimuli. Logically, emotion to some degree promotes or hinders the amount of energy available to gain information. As this innate feature of the human condition unfolds, adults develop a variety of emotion-based mental images to guide their actions. These ongoing thoughts act as the foundation and sense of order needed to continue the activities of daily living. An example is sometimes witnessed when two individuals marry. For some couples, a preconceived idea of a perfect wedding guides their selection of the setting, music, flowers, and honeymoon. As they begin their life journey, images of themselves and those around them act as the basis for their first home, vacations, child-rearing practices, and daily events. As this couple matures the way in which they adapt and adjust their hopes, dreams, and desires (images) will determine if they nurture or oppress their own and each other's innate talents.

When thinking further about mental images, Kubler-Ross's

(1969) stages of death and dying might explain how individuals respond and ultimately change their thinking. Initially, adults deny that their thoughts are incongruent with reality and impossible to achieve in the future. As time passes, they become angry when realizing that regardless of their efforts, they will not experience what is included within their mental image. For some, they will bargain with a higher power to gain the necessary support needed. When denial, anger, and bargaining fail, the individual becomes depressed prior to accepting that their hopes, dreams, and desires in life will not come to fruition. Once reaching this point, they have the opportunity to change their way of thinking while simultaneously nurturing their talent.

Emotion often hinders the ability to alter thoughts. In many instances, adults have a tendency to blame someone else rather than accepting that their ideas and actions may contribute to why they are unable to obtain their hopes, dreams, and desires. It appears easier to cope with difficulties when fault is placed on your parents, spouse, or some other specific event. In spite of what Freud (1938) and other like-minded individuals have suggested, it is hard to believe that most daily struggles and perceived difficulties can be traced to the first few years of life. It seems more likely that adults inadvertently oppress themselves simply due to their genetic makeup, along with how they have been conditioned to respond to the daily activities of living. This form of self-oppression could be measured by the statement, "I do not have a choice." The frequency and intensity of emotion exhibited during its occurrence may reflect the amount of energy spent in emotional discomfort. Logically, the greater the length of time in emotional disharmony, the less likely some desired outcome will result.

A review of the human indoctrination process might also help to determine how emotion affects the activities of daily living.

Life's journey begins within an existing culture containing mores and values that provide the sense of order needed to feel safe and secure. Families, places of worship, schools, and media then immerse the developing child with information. In most instances, an individual's need for belonging results in the acceptance of ideas without question. As life progresses, what is perceived as truth may not be accurate thoughts but rather the accumulation of preexisting beliefs. In many cases, this feature of the human condition presents itself in statements such as "If you work hard, you will have a higher quality of life." For some that may be true; however, for others a causal relationship between effort and outcome has little impact on the quality of life. A number of interrelated, multifaceted outcomes also seem to result from the indoctrination process. The most obvious is that creative thought may not be valued. Children and adults who have ideas that cause others discomfort often are judged, avoided and isolated. In extreme cases, various labels are assigned and interventions implemented in order to promote a sense of safety and a level of conformity. As this occurs, a hierarchical structure develops with certain individuals perceived as valuable while others are devalued.

The indoctrination process may be further illuminated using a tunnel example. The width of the tunnel represents the mores and values of society and the length is average life expectancy. As individuals enter the tunnel (birth) others (mother, father, and siblings) begin to bombard them with information and specific actions to shape their present and future way of thinking. As individuals muddle and plod along within the tunnel, their emotional needs cause them to remain without question. If they do try to temporarily or permanently leave, others attempt to pull them back using traditional beliefs, laws and physical force. For those who do escape, they are often thought of as deficit in something, labeled, and in need of support. Once they gain assistance (usually medical), it is generally believed that they will realize the error in their ways and reenter the tunnel. For those who still resist, they will often be perceived as dangerous and in need of constant supervision and oversight. What is also noticed is that in the past and still today, the dimensions of the tunnel seem to act paradoxically. The width and length provides the sense of order needed for some to identify and nurture one's talent while for others it acts to oppress innate talent. It too seems relatively clear that in order for talent to be identified and nurtured, the dimensions of the tunnel have to become wider veering in various directions.

CHAPTER SUMMARY

This chapter explored emotion and human talent. Emotion to some degree appears to nurture or oppress human capital. Human capital is thought of as not only a bank account, a thousand shares of General Electric stock, but also competence, knowledge, and personality attributes embodied in the ability to perform labor of economic value (Becker, 1993, Sullivan, and Sheffrin, 2003). Specific human capital further refers to skills or knowledge that is useful only to a single employer or industry, whereas general human capital (such as literacy) is useful to all employers. In spite of these traditional definitions and various theories involving human capital, collective and individual talents go beyond those which might be easily identified or measured.

Human growth and development areas were used to explore how emotion impacts human talent. A number of outcomes were thought to occur when emotion impacts physical, cognitive, social, and moral development. The most obvious is that individuals divide themselves into smaller self-defined groups, distinct and separate from the larger population. Adults too instinctively gravitate toward others who share common characteristics and similar beliefs. The sense of belonging and camaraderie gained from this typical action seems to provide the foundation for psychological health. However, it may also result in emotional stagnation, self-oppression, and divisiveness within and between various groups of people. Individuals in this state of discomfort usually demonstrate patterns of behavior indicating they feel as though they have little control in their life and they are victims of something. To offset these intense feelings, most actions regardless of the individual, are to some degree self-serving.

An attempt was then made to answer the question why certain innate talents remain dormant while others are activated and cultivated. It was suggested that to some degree, the experiences within the family, school, and information from the media shape human talent. This life-altering process begins with the type and frequency of interaction occurring between an infant and their care provider. As children become older, parenting styles along with information gained while at school and through the media act to nurture or hinder native talent. It was suggested that the probability in which innate talent surfaces and is cultivated, depends on the emotional well-being of those involved. In the end, emotion is a natural aspect of life that promotes innate talent for some while limiting others.

EMOTION'S IMPACT ON POLICY DEVELOPMENT AND IMPLEMENTATION

Policy development and implementation is another example of how human emotion lessens the probability of individual and collective change. Werner (2002) indicated that a policy reflects a set of guiding values and principles used to design programs and strategic plans. Individuals who create policies are often thought of as policy scientists. These professionals typically adopt a lawyer's or doctor's practice as their model, putting the methods and findings to work solving real-world problems (Lasswell, 1971). The policy scientist is also considered a strategic innovative expert in intelligence who is comfortable communicating information to various audiences to answer fundamental questions of concern. As for science, policy scientists embrace the ideas of generalization and objectivity with preference given to problem-driven contextual models and quantification (Farr, Hacker, and Kazee, 2006).

Lasswell (1958 and 1965) also suggested that the overriding goal of policy in our body politic required becoming "life-centered, not man-centered." Political scientists are obligated to study collective policy choices that could ultimately affect millions of people and divide societies. This life-centered approach naturally includes the intricacies and complexities of human emotion.

COMMUNICATION: THE VEHICLE OF EMOTION

The emotions conveyed through various communication patterns shape the content and the manner in which policies are developed and implemented. Communication is thought of as a complex symbol system that conveys meaning between individuals and groups. In spite of its nuances and intricacies, verbal language to some degree seems to be simply a multifaceted process used to meet basic human needs. For instance, when children and adults label an object, condition, or other intangible entity or phenomenon they gain a sense of safety and security. An example is sometimes noticed when someone has a physical ailment that is creating difficulty. As discomfort persists, a feeling of lack of control surfaces and at times manifests into a level of fear and anxiety that is often worse than the actual symptom. Sometimes, even in the most horrific situation, patients gain comfort by obtaining information regarding their medical condition. Another need-based language illustration is how some adults respond when items are not labeled or organized. In many cases, they become uneasy and afraid of things that are different. Consider for instance how adults might react if they enter a local grocery or department store without any obvious product organization. They would usually be overwhelmed and leave the store.

Language-based theoretical constructs are also created to offset fear and other related uncomfortable feelings. Alfred Binet for example was commissioned by the government of France to devise measures to determine the ability of school children and members of the military (Binet and Simon, 1916). After a series of lengthy experiments, Binet coined the term *intelligence* to describe and quantify human ability and aptitude. He would later travel to Stanford University in California where his test became known as the Stanford-Binet Test of Intelligence. Over a hundred years later, the term *intelligence* is now a constant cultural fixture used in decision making. Another example occurred in 1944, Hans Asperger, an Austrian pediatrician, identified and labeled clusters of human behavior as Asperger's syndrome. Children experiencing this condition can verbally communicate but exhibit patterns of social skill deficits that hinder learning, relationship development, and future employment opportunities (Firth, 1991).

As new disciplines emerge, they normally develop their own terminology in order to create and promote their professional identity. An example is the field of special education, an education subspecialty focusing on children with disabilities. Initially, children with disabilities were thought of as those with physical deformities or mental retardation. As time passed, hidden disabilities such as learning and emotional difficulties were identified. Still today, an ongoing debate exists as to what human characteristics comprise a certain category of variance. For instance, the category and label of autism has now changed to autism spectrum disorders. Along with definitional difficulties, the terms "individualized education program," "prereferral," and "least restrictive environment" provide evidence of how specialization results in discipline specific language. Another more familiar example is the field of medicine. Each subspecialty has its own unique vocabulary and procedures that require extensive formal training.

When you further think about language and policy development and implementation, it is important to consider how words have multiple meanings and connotations. Many of the connotations associated with certain terms reflect how emotion impacts understanding, personal relationships, and the activities of daily living. For instance, if adults have had their electricity turned off, went without food, or did not have anywhere to sleep, they will respond differently. Human emotion is embedded in each life experience and is conveyed through the meanings and connotations assigned to words or phrases.

The emotions associated with certain words are shaped by many variables. The most obvious is tradition. Traditions affect the communication patterns within families, schools, employment settings, and places of worship. Geographic location is another aspect influencing the meaning and connotations of words. For example, differences exist between the southern and northern United States. In the southern United States, "It is flooding over here" indicates that a thunderstorm is occurring. In the northern United States, the same statement would mean that a river has crested over its bank and water is flowing along or over the road into homes. Other words and phrases such as *yous*, *fixin'*, *soda*, *pop*, and "I carried him and his friends to the park" indicate regional differences. The media in its role as the contemporary "bully pulpit" as well influences and shapes the meaning and connotations of words. For instance, when certain individuals such as entertainers, athletes, scholars, and politicians speak, listeners frequently adopt similar thoughts and communication patterns. It is also clear that the context and the frequency in which the media convey certain words or phrases guide how others use them. Statements such as "It is what it is," and "What is the takeaway are examples of how the media subtly molds the communication patterns of children and adults.

Nonverbal language is another aspect of communication impacting policy development and implementation. Nonverbal messages consist of physical movements or actions that covey meaning such as eye contact, hand gestures, body positioning, facial expressions, and physical proximity. It appears that within any human interaction, emotion impacts the type of nonverbal message sent and its interpretation. For instance, when a group of individuals are at a local restaurant, subtle nonverbal actions to some degree promote or hinder the quality of the experience. Within this intricately unique human process, nonverbal communication patterns are shaped by subconscious thoughts and emotions. The real question perhaps though is how standards of nonverbal behavior are established. In some situations, it seems that regardless of the message conveyed, an individual might be perceived as rude or another similar negative term simply due to the fact that someone may not physically feel very well.

The emotions conveyed through various language patterns promote or hinder the level of emotional intimacy felt between people. Emotional intimacy can be defined as a sense of closeness that results from the sharing of important personal thoughts and experiences. As one might expect, individuals struggle with intimacy due to their basic survival instinct to avoid vulnerability and harm. A common outcome of this is that most children and adults gravitate toward others who either are physically, intellectually, and emotionally similar to them. An example is sometimes noticed when a person new to the community is invited to a party. As they enter the social situation, they seem awkward and uncomfortable as they move from one existing group to the next until they find others whom they are comfortable with. For many, limited emotional intimacy seems to result in a search for group identity rather than their own. A preexisting category, such as lawyers, engineers, teachers, and criminals, provides an emotionally safe arena in which to function. As this typical emotion-based response occurs, individuals may inadvertently oppress themselves by not interacting with others who have different interests and thoughts that ultimately could enhance their quality of life.

When adults lack emotional intimacy in their life, they seem concerned with what others think about them. Individuals with this mind-set usually determine their value in comparison to others rather than their own unique criteria for self-worth. For example in most capitalistic societies, a large home, expensive car, or other material possession is perceived as successful. In actuality, someone may be "house poor," unable to enjoy their home because they work many hours to afford the monthly mortgage. Another example is marriage. Many couples compare their experiences or lifestyle to others. Statements such as "They appear so happy. Are we as happy as they are?" or "Why can't you be more like Tom?" make this evident. A norm-referenced life perspective may explain too why competition is rampant between individuals and groups. Competition in general does not seem to promote emotional intimacy but rather creates fear, anxiety, and a high level of mistrust.

In summary, policy development and implementation is impacted by the emotions conveyed through various communication patterns. As children and adults respond to environmental stimuli, emotion more so than intellect determines nonverbal and verbal communication patterns. All behavior therefore is a communicative attempt to satisfy to some degree a basic human need. It is also clear that within any culture, words gain multiple meanings based on tradition, location of residency, and the context and frequency of use by the media. Communication is the vehicle of emotion that influences human relationships, ultimately impacting the design and implementation of policies.

EMOTION, LEARNING, AND DEPTH OF UNDERSTANDING

The policies that are developed and implemented reflect emotion's impact on learning and depth of understanding. Learning is often thought of as acquiring, comprehending, and using information to solve real-life problems (Skinner and Belmont, 1993). The total amount of knowledge of a particular topic is usually referred to as depth of understanding. A simplistic example is someone learning to play tennis. They begin with how to hold the racket to hit groundstrokes, and progress to play competitive matches with friends. With instruction, time and extensive practice, the individual will transition from a beginner to tournament level player. It too appears that how the tennis player feels at particular points in time will determine the rate in which they will progress in their abilities.

Human emotions seem to frequently hinder learning. An example is sometimes noticed when observing two individuals in a conversation. When one person creates a sense of uneasiness for the other, the listener to some degree becomes unable to hear or comprehend what is being said because their basic survival instincts are activated. Further observation reveals that subtle nonverbal messages are then usually conveyed to change the topic or end the conversation, thus preventing participants from gaining information that could enhance their depth of understanding. Another variable influencing learning is the frequency and intensity of previous emotional violations. For instance, if a teenager was bullied by his peers in elementary school he may feel awkward in social settings. In extreme cases, high levels of anxiety may cause him to become very withdrawn unwilling to interact with almost everyone. Also evident is how temporary fluctuations in emotions influence someone's ability to obtain information at a given point in time. An example perhaps is when your mind begins to wonder from a task; emotion rather than intellect appears as the logical reason why this happens.

Emotion as well causes adults to be hesitant and reluctant to read and accept information that conflicts with their existing ideas or thoughts. Many individuals seem emotionally trapped, comfortable with sameness and routine. An example of this occurred when a university professor was observing a student intern. The prospective teacher was presenting a reading lesson to a group of children with complex learning needs. The students along with the supervisor struggled maintaining attention to the lesson; the instruction was clearly insensitive to the needs of the learner and was simply boring. At the end of the class period, a debriefing session was held to provide feedback and suggestions to make the lesson more intriguing. What was interesting was how the student intern responded. He stated, "I have never seen these strategies, so I am not sure they work." His thinking clearly was inaccurate; however, it may reflect how his emotions caused him to believe that his lesson was acceptable and that it had promoted student learning. Now that we have briefly mentioned how individuals are reluctant to accept information that conflicts with their own thoughts; it might be helpful to consider how cognitive skills develop in order to uncover how emotions impact depth of understanding and policy development.

Piaget (1937) suggested that cognitive development takes place in four distinct stages: sensorimotor, preoperational, concrete operational, and formal operational. Each stage builds on previous experiences, beginning with infants acting on the world with their eyes, ears, and hands and ending with adolescence and adults able to solve abstract problems. Despite Piaget's complex ideas and delineations, human emotion may cause individuals to remain at the concrete operational stage, unable to process and understand abstract information. Many adults for instance seem to need to directly experience something before they understand a certain concept. What also appears evident is how increased access to information creates a general attitude among some people that they have a high level of knowledge on a particular topic when they do not. A consequence of this contemporary reality is a general sense of uneasiness between and among people. This is sometimes reflected in statements such as "They know just enough to be dangerous."

A number of consequences result when emotion affects abstract thinking. The most obvious is that individuals are gullible, easily fooled to believe the latest fads in medicine, finance, and education. Also, an inability to consistently think abstractly causes many adults to make assumptions as to what is true or might happen. For example in an employment setting, some individuals feel that if they state a contradictory point of view they might lose their job. In actuality, a certain level of stress may result that is detrimental to their health if they do not express their ideas. Another outcome of limited abstract thinking is the reliance on a quantitative perspective of reality. Almost every aspect of daily life seems based on measurement as numbers provide a tangible means to gain a sense of order. Numbers in and of themselves do not have meaning; however, the emotion-based values placed on them significantly influence decision making. For example, the number of students not finishing high school troubles many members of society. This issue of concern is an emotional talking point highlighting the problems youth are experiencing in school and the difficulties employers are having locating qualified employees. The historical emphasis placed on

Gallup Polls provides further evidence of the role of quantitative data on public discourse and policy development.

Human emotion clearly impacts the level of knowledge available for the design and implementation of policies. In many instances, it appears that how an individual feels at a particular point in time determines how much information might be gained, understood, and remembered. The reason for this can be attributed to the protective functions emotions play in life. Emotions to some degree innately act as buffers or defense mechanisms to avoid discomfort and pain. It also appears that as this uniquely human process unfolds, most adults unintentionally are reluctant to take intellectual risks as they surround themselves with people and ideas similar to their own. Emotions as well cause many adults to make decisions that are detrimental to their life.

EMOTION AND POLICY DEVELOPMENT AND IMPLEMENTATION

Lasswell's (1971) seven general policy questions will be used as the conceptual framework to explore how emotion impacts policy development and implementation. Each question will be stated, and the role and impact of emotion will be discussed.

1. Whose policy goals are to be realized?

The first step in examining policy alternatives is to make sure that explicit assumptions are made about the identity of the decision makers (Lasswell, 1971). As you consider this question, *power* is a term that comes to mind. The individual or group who has the greatest level of influence will determine the policy goals that are established. For instance, the United States Constitution describes the roles of the three branches of government. Despite the wisdom of the founding fathers, human emotion to some degree ultimately determines who is and is not perceived as powerful. Historically, skilled hunters and gatherers were valued due to the need to survive. Today, individuals who are born into certain families, obtain monetary wealth, and attend Ivy League schools receive elevated social standing. It appears that when certain members of society are perceived with higher status than others, a general sense of competition and inequality arises. Another emotion-based social status example is found with entertainers who have children that experience disabilities. Their physical appearance or role in a recent movie or television show allows them to have a forum to share their experiences when others do not.

Socioeconomic status also impacts the policy goals to be realized. For example, Kozol (1991), in his book *Savage Inequalities*, described the condition of neighborhoods, public services, and schools throughout the United States. His descriptive accounts highlight the differences between the "haves and have nots." A vicious cycle of poverty clearly exists as generations of individuals (have nots) have limited upward mobility due to their constant struggle to obtain basic necessities, such as food, adequate shelter, and educational opportunities. In contrast, those with resources (haves) have greater influence on individuals and groups that design policies. Typically, their energy is used to promote their own self-interests.

2. What is the problem or set of problems in hand?

A problem is a discrepancy between goals and an actual or anticipated state of affairs (Lasswell, 1971). Issues identified as problems are normally based on an emotion-based set of values. Maslow's (1943) hierarchy of needs is a possible way to explain why certain environmental events are perceived as problems and others are not. He suggested that physiological needs are at the bottom of the hierarchy, followed in ascending order by safety, belongingness and love, esteem, and self-actualization. The lower the need is, the greater its strength. When a lower-level need is activated, such as extreme hunger or fear for one's physical safety, children and adults stop trying to satisfy a higher-level desire (Maslow, 1987). As this innate emotion-based response continues and evolves into discomfort and pain, what is occurring at that particular moment is often perceived as a problem.

Primitive survival instincts also seem to naturally create an "in-to-out perspective" regarding problems. For instance, the closer the issue is to the life of the majority of individuals, the more likely it is perceived as a problem. As you move further away, less emphasis is placed on the matter as it is not perceived as an issue of concern. An example of this is crime. Most adults accept that crime exists; however, it is only considered a problem when it consistently happens in your neighborhood. Emotion as well causes many children and adults to naturally become self-centered in order to protect themselves from perceived harm. This fear and general sense of uneasiness is also fueled by repeated negative images conveyed through the media, such as the bridge collapse in Minnesota or the number of parents harming their children. In all aspects of human life, a problem appears to be determined based more so on a set of emotion-laden values rather than intellectual thoughts.

3. What particularized objectives are realized through the policy process

Policy outcomes are determined based on the perceptions of those who design and benefit directly from them (Lasswell,

1971). A logical question therefore is whether the policy obtains intended outcomes or it benefits a few to the detriment of the majority. It appears that the intensity of emotional discomfort and pain associated with a problem determines the rate of response. When the majority of citizens are impacted or select powerful few, actions seem to be swift. Recent examples of collective emotional uneasiness are found in the reaction to issues related to national security and the maltreatment of children and animals throughout the world.

Specific policy objectives are influenced by the emotion-laden values of those participating in decision making. What is considered valuable is based on a variety of contextual variables such as history, human capital, and existing cultural attitudes. An example of this is the recent discussions associated with marijuana. Some states have passed laws supporting the medical use of marijuana as others have been hesitant to accept the scientific evidence of its benefits. Other similar emotion-based quagmires seem to be present when discussing topics such as basic human rights, obscenity laws, bullying, and economic policies. How a problem is defined as well determines the logical order in which solutions are conceptualized and developed and resources are allocated. An important consideration in this often linear process is for individuals to be aware of how subconscious and conscious emotional states impact their problem-solving abilities.

4. Assuming the objective can be realized, what is the probability that they will optimize the results?

When determining if policy objectives optimize results, it is important to consider how emotion impacts measurement and evaluation. Genetics, along with the many emotions associated with the human indoctrination process, explains why individuals differ in the way in which they perceive the outcomes of a shared experience. Human emotions also often determine the selection of a criterion or norm-referenced evaluation tool. Criterion-referenced measures evaluate performance based on a preestablished standard; norm-referenced evaluation tools compare individual actions to others who are similar in some way. To clarify the difference between the two common evaluation perspectives, it might be helpful to consider how someone receives a driver's license in the United States. In most states, individuals have to meet a certain criterion-referenced standard on a written exam and demonstrate proficiency driving an automobile. Their score is not a reflection of their performance compared to others but rather is based on a predetermined standard. Regardless of the choice of methodology, emotion impacts the perception, reporting, and evaluation of results.

Policy objectives in most cases also appear to be designed based on an egocentric point of view. When individuals perceive actions as promoting their self-interest, they are more likely to support the policy. This typical way of thinking is perhaps linked to basic survival needs. For instance, emotions naturally act as buffers and protective barriers that cause individuals to first consider their needs rather than those of others. As this occurs, response differences sometimes create an emotional spiraling effect where certain individuals and groups regardless of policy content perceive the outcome as not beneficial to them. Human emotion is clearly self-serving, and in many instances, it acts to divide people into categories or boxes based on the primitive need for safety and security.

5. What decisions are most adequate to obtain the desired outcomes?

Institutional leaders communicate core values as they design policies and procedures that promote desired outcomes. As one would expect then, individual leadership styles are important to consider. Hersey and Blanchard (1988) identified three common leadership styles that reflect the emotional needs of the leader. An autocratic leader is involved in almost all decisions regardless of their significance. They often lead by communicating in ways that create fear in their employees. In contrast, a laissez-faire leader is typically perceived as having little or no emotional investment in the activities of the organization. Between these extremes is an authoritative leader. This type of leadership style is thought to balance the emotional needs of the leader and employees. Shared decision making is frequently present in this approach. It appears, however, that when leaders reach a certain level of self-awareness, they are able to identify and assess the emotional needs of others. When this happens, work environments are usually created that nurture and empower innate human potential to obtain desired outcomes.

An additional variable impacting outcomes is the hiring and placement of employees in positions that maximize their ability. Corporations with consistent policies and procedures governing hiring, induction, assessment, and evaluation, are more likely to identify and employ individuals with certain skill sets that promote valued outcomes. A key emotion-based element of this process is for leaders to identify their biases and how these perspectives impact decision making. An example is when an employer is friends with certain employees. Their shared experiences and personal relationships may act as an emotional barrier, preventing the accurate identification and assessment of employee abilities. Hiring and promotion practices that are shaped by emotion-based thoughts significantly affect results.

6. What predispositions are favorable, unfavorable, or noncommittal in reference to the outcomes as presently formulated?

When determining favorable and unfavorable predispositions that promote desired outcomes, it is important to consider how emotion impacts the existing context. An example is an employment setting. If an atmosphere of caring, trust, and shared decision making exists, positive outcomes seem to result. In contrast, if competition promotes mistrust and a lack of unity, negative consequences sometimes occur, such as low employee morale, high turnover rates, and a general lack of productivity. One could also suggest that if employees feel a sense of purpose and joy from their efforts rather than simply trying to gain an income, they are more likely to expend energy in ways that promote the obtainment of desired outcomes.

Another consideration impacting outcomes is the level of individual compensation. Despite altruistic thoughts, most adults work in order to obtain the resources necessary to maintain a certain lifestyle. If someone feels as though they are not paid enough, their actions sometimes hinder the obtainment of desired results. For instance, they may have limited loyalty to the institution or perform only at a level that allows them to maintain their job rather than using all the skills in which they possess. To offset this typical emotion-based response, leaders frequently develop processes in which they share decision making authority with employees. It appears that when individuals feel their input is valued, they lessen their negative feelings associated with a lack of pay. For this enhanced problem-solving dialogue and shared decision making to continue, leaders must first have a general understanding of how emotion impacts self-perception.

7. What strategies will optimize value goals?

Communication mediums shape the perception of desired outcomes while optimizing value goals. It too appears that the timing and format in which policies are disseminated influence the emotional reaction of those impacted. When a policy affects a large number of people, the distribution process usually consists of a written document followed by an individual spokesperson discussing the issue of concern. Naturally, the characteristics of the person conveying the information, and the subtle messages sent through the use of color, charts, and video often determines the type and intensity of the emotional response. Logically, the more extreme the action is perceived as, the greater the emotional response. Another communication strategy optimizing value goals is the frequency in which information is expressed. Repeated exposure seems to result in the acceptance of ideas that previously were shocking and confusing. This new information merely becomes engrained as part of the normal way of life.

The selection and the way in which goods and services are used reflect value goals. When policy developers detail comprehensive long- and short-term resource allocation guidelines, positive outcomes often result. As this typical planning process develops and evolves, the personal perspectives of decision makers influence how goods and services are used. What also seems to occur is that intangible attributes such as employee attitudes, motivation, and relationships are influenced more by emotion than certain tangible goods. An example is the perception and use of time. Human emotion creates a sense of urgency causing many adults to adopt a short-term rather than long-term perspective in decision making. This common emotion-based reaction significantly shapes the content and implementation of policies.

When reviewing Lasswell's (1971) seven policy questions, it is clear that human emotion to some degree affects policy development and implementation. Many individuals for instance would still not have the opportunity to vote, participate in religious activities, or gain access to public and private institutions without the energy gained from emotion-based societal movements and collective actions. Emotion more so than intellect also determines the content and way in which policies are developed and implemented. It appears that in spite of emotions significant power in decision making, many individuals do not seem to realize its impact on the activities of daily living. To illuminate and perhaps offset this oversight, a review of the many emotion-based issues associated with autism spectrum disorders follows.

HUMAN EMOTION AND AUTISM SPECTRUM DISORDERS

The field of autism spectrum disorders is influenced by the emotions of political leaders, community members, educators, and parents. Examples of this are reflected in some of the current issues related to the identification, early intervention, educational curriculum, and transition to adulthood of students with autism spectrum disorders.

IDENTIFICATION

The identification of children experiencing autism spectrum disorders is impacted by the availability of information. Many parents, after reading various Internet articles seem afraid that their child will demonstrate patterns of behavior labeled along the autism spectrum. As one mother recently stated, "My maternal instincts to protect my child causes me to be hypersensitive as I continually look for signs of autism. I wonder if my child is developing normally or if there is something wrong." Media reports of the numbers of children experiencing autism spectrum disorders as well create high levels of anxiety among parents and guardians.

Another emotion-based identification issue is noticed when adults search for absolute answers rather than a range of options. An example is the reliance on developmental milestones to guide decision making. Developmental milestones specify the chronological age in which a child is to exhibit certain behaviors such as crawling, walking, and verbally communicating. If a youngster is not ambulatory by his first birthday, a level of concern may arise needlessly when he walks at fourteen months of age. The parental need for definitive answers increases the likelihood of error in the diagnosis of children with autism spectrum disorders.

EARLY INTERVENTION

After a child is identified as experiencing autism spectrum disorders, the emotional response of some parents and guardians becomes an obstacle in obtaining necessary supports. Parents in many instances seem to exhibit emotion-based behaviors that parallel three of Kubler Ross's (1969) stages of death and dying. Initially, they deny their child has autism because no apparent physical differences exist. They struggle with the idea their youngster is unlike other children because they perceive themselves as similar to everyone else. Denying and rejecting the diagnosis of autism spectrum disorders allows parents to escape the reality that they too may be different from those around them.

When the difficulties associated with autism persist, many parents become angry. Family members, health professionals, and early intervention specialists are often targets of the parents' rage, resentment, and envy of those who have children not experiencing autism spectrum disorders. For many parents, their anger distorts perception, creating a stressful atmosphere that negatively affects health, marriage, and employment. What appears difficult and perhaps fuels the anger for many parents is that certain experiences they envisioned with their child will not occur. For instance, a father's image of playing catch in the backyard with his son or working together in the family business may not materialize. The sadness associated with relinquishing previously held hopes, dreams, and desires may cause parents to experience varying levels of depression. With time and emotional support, many parents reach a point where they will accept that their child experiences autism spectrum disorders.

EDUCATIONAL CURRICULUM

The curricular experiences of students with autism spectrum disorders are determined by the knowledge and attitudes of parents and educators. It seems relatively clear that many of the difficulties in curriculum decision making exist because of the variability among student skill levels and the lack of consensus as to what children with autism spectrum disorders are capable of learning. With limited definitive research to guide current practice, the emotions related to individual human differences, pity, and empowerment impact the school experiences of students with autism spectrum disorders.

Despite legislation promoting free and appropriate public education, many members of society appear to pity those with autism spectrum disorders. Individuals seem to feel sorry for children and adults who have significant skills deficits. For example, in some parts of the United States, evidence of this is reflected in statements such as "Bless his heart," or "It takes a special person to work with disabled kids." A common outcome of this emotion-based way of thinking is that many students are perceived as incapable, in need of extensive constant assistance, while simultaneously being denied educational opportunities. Education curriculums should then logically focus on the development of skills that ultimately empower individuals to be self-determined as they participate in the activities of daily living. For this to occur, professional development is essential to explore and identify the emotion-based assumptions many educators have regarding the education of students with autism spectrum disorders. Special emphasis should be placed on creating learning opportunities that require educators to explore their attitudes towards individuals who are different from them.

TRANSITION TO ADULTHOOD

The transition of youth with autism spectrum disorders from school to adulthood poses a challenge. It appears that when local community members have few interactions with youth with disabilities, their emotion-based perceptions and actions sometimes hinder post-school success. Those with limited understanding also seem to assume that all individuals with autism spectrum disorders are incapable of living independently, gaining meaningful employment, and contributing positively to society. In contrast, if local business owners gain knowledge of the many abilities of youth with autism spectrum disorders, they are more likely to accept their differences in hiring practices. It is clear that education and religious leaders need to convey positive messages regarding student abilities in order to increase the post-school success of youth with autism spectrum disorders.

State and local agencies serving individuals with disabilities have a significant effect on the post-school success of youth with autism spectrum disorders. Community agencies receiving ongoing financial support appear to become a permanent fixture providing a variety of valuable services. An additional consideration is the amount of money available to compensate agency employees. If constant streams of funding are available skilled professionals are more likely hired and retained. If not, low employee retention rates increase hiring and induction costs ultimately hindering the effectiveness of the agency. Lastly and most importantly are the attitudes of agency employees directly interacting with individuals experiencing autism spectrum disorders. If empowering perspectives rather than thoughts of pity exist, comprehensive programs are more likely designed.

Parents experience a variety of emotion-based transition concerns when their child with autism spectrum disorders needs constant ongoing support. The most difficult issue appears to be who will provide care for their child when they are no longer able or present. The anxiety associated with the future as well naturally creates high levels of stress and a sense of hopelessness for many parents. It is also evident that even when families agree that certain individuals will care for the adult with autism spectrum disorders, emotional uneasiness exists. These ongoing difficulties associated with providing lifelong custodial care results in a variety of legal, financial, and family issues.

CHAPTER SUMMARY

This chapter explored how policy development and implementation is influenced by the intricacies and complexities of human emotion. Emotion consists of complex layers of processes that are in constant contact with the environment. At a minimum, these interactions include cognitive stimuli appraisal or evaluation of meaning and physical changes such as endocrine, autonomic, and cardiovascular. Various emotions are naturally reflected in the communication process in which policies are developed and implemented. Communication consists of a complex nonverbal and verbal symbol system that conveys meaning between individuals and groups. Emotion, more so than intellect, also causes many words and actions to have multiple meaning and connotations. This aspect of the human condition impacts most, if not all, activities of daily living.

Lasswell's (1971) seven general policy questions were then used to explore how emotion impacts policy development and implementation. It was clearly evident that without the energy gained from emotion-based societal movement and collective actions, many individuals would still not have the opportunity to vote, participate in religious activities, or gain access to public and private institutions. It was also suggested that despite a general awareness of emotion, many individuals do not seem to realize its influence on the aspects of daily life. To conclude the chapter, a brief discussion of autism spectrum disorder was provided to further illuminate how emotion not only impacts broad issues of concern and their related policies but also a human condition that is becoming more prevalent in society. In the upcoming chapter, additional observations will be explored in order to determine how emotion is reflected in specific actions.

EMOTION'S IMPACT ON BEHAVIOR

Throughout history, members of various civilizations have established behavioral norms for certain environmental contexts. These standards provide the foundation to meet the emotional need for safety and security. A simplistic example is noticed when considering leisure activities. For instance, if an audience member at a play yelled at a performer as they commonly do at a football referee, they would be asked to change their actions or leave. Why does that typically occur? Who determined that it was acceptable to yell at a referee and not an actor? In other instances, if children and adults consistently challenge the behavioral norms, they are thought of as experiencing attention-deficit hyperactivity disorder (ADHD), obsessive-compulsive disorder (OCD), or oppositional defiant disorder (ODD). A question that naturally arises then is, what variables ultimately decide situational conduct norms?

Emotion more so than intellect determines what behavior is considered appropriate in certain contexts. These internal feelings range from primitive reflexes to multifaceted complexities labeled and described as happiness, anger, joy, sadness, guilt, fear, hope, and love. In this chapter, special emphasis will be placed on why some individuals have the ability to adapt their behavior to meet the demands of certain contextual variables and others do not. An alternative explanation for behavior will also be provided.

EMOTION AND THE DEVELOPMENT OF BEHAVIORAL NORMS

Individuals learn responses by observing and listening to others around them (Bandura, 1977) . A baby who claps his hands for instance after his father does so or a child who angrily hits a playmate the same way they have been punished demonstrate how environmental variables impact human behavior. Beginning at birth, interactions between an infant and adult have a profound impact on the developing child. For example, adult models paired with cues and prompts from care providers help the child meet their basic need for personal safety. Bandura (1986) also implied that the emotions associated with certain experiences within the family, places of worship, school, and information gained through the media impact and shape behavioral patterns. A brief examination of these socializing agents might be helpful to explore how behavioral norms are typically established.

FAMILIES

American families are different today than they were a few decades ago. Currently, about half of all families are based on a first marriage. In other situations, a single parent heads almost one-third; the remainder is remarriages or some other arrangement (Insel and Roth, 2000). Also, in 2003, 68 percent of children under age eighteen lived with two married parents, 23 percent lived with their mothers, five percent with fathers, and four percent with someone other than their parents (Federal Interagency Forum on Child and Family Statistics, 2004). As one might then expect, a family's emotional well-being is impacted by divorce. For instance, at any given time, over one million American youth experience the separation of their parents as approximately one- fourth of youngsters live in single-parent households (Meyer and Garasky, 1993). Children during the process of divorce, sometimes emotionally react by becoming angry or withdrawing from their less secure home lives. Some blame themselves for their family difficulties as they experience a state of confusion, uneasiness, and fear of the unknown. Another factor thought to influence a child's behavior is the length of time that the marital relationship struggled prior to termination. During this difficult period, children are physically present but often perceived through a hurting frame of reference, causing them to sometimes have their needs overlooked. Many children as well appear lost as they try to make sense of their world without the skills to understand what is happening to their mom and dad.

After the divorce, child custody options impact the behavioral patterns of children. In joint guardianship, the courts grant the mother and father equal input in important decisions about the child's upbringing. In most instances, children reside with one parent and visit the other on a fixed schedule; in other cases, physical custody is shared as children move between homes and sometimes schools and peer groups (Johnston, Kline, and Tschann, 1989). Parents as well normally experience a self-exploration and validation process after the divorce. Initially, some state, "I will never get married again," as they place protective barriers or walls around them to recover from the psychological violations that happened during their marriage. As time passes, friends and other members of the community usually encourage them to participate in social events and date again. During this period, children may feel abandoned and hopeless as they struggle to gain the emotional support they need. If remarriage does occur, a host of blended family issues arise such as role clarification, parenting styles, communication patterns, and personal loyalty. The structure and dynamics of families have changed due to divorce; however, they still have a significant affect on the actions and emotional well-being of youth.

PLACES OF WORSHIP

Places of worship provide the spiritual and emotional context to determine what actions are appropriate and inappropriate. As youth become older, they normally adopt their parents' belief system or gravitate toward institutions that represent their ideas. This common pattern of behavior has resulted in Christian typologies (McLaren, 2004) ranging from Conservative Protestants to Liberation Theology. Within each group there is a variety of nuances, substreams, counter-streams, weaknesses, problems and minority opinions as evidenced by the differing interpretations of content within the same denomination (McLaren, 2004). Regardless of the differences in general viewpoint between and within generations of each religious sect, human actions typically reflect the emotions associated with certain beliefs.

In spite of the moral absolutes gained from places of worship, individuals often experience subconscious and conscious thoughts that contradict with their religious training. For many, these ideas result in unsettling emotions. This ongoing struggle causes some to seek counseling or obtain medication to help them perform better in the eyes of a higher power. Many others seem to avoid thinking about their religious foundation as they simply rationalize their behavior based on their own interpretation of the Bible or some other religious doctrine. An example of this sometimes occurs when a corporate leader emphasizes productivity to the detriment of workers. He constantly requires his employees to become more productive as attempts are made to decrease costs. In his ongoing quest for material wealth, decisions are often made that result in low wages and limited employee benefits. As the corporation and individual economic situation becomes more prosperous, he rationalizes his behavior by making statements such as "I am creating jobs for people" and "With the money I earn, I donate to all these worthy causes including a large proportion to my church." Regardless of the many rationalizations used to justify behavior, the emotions associated with certain experiences within places of worship have a significant impact on behavior.

SCHOOLS

At the heart of any society is an education commitment that affords members the opportunity to stretch their minds to full capacity. Education is important because of not only what it contributes to individuals but also the value added to the general quality of life within communities. Two teaching approaches have historically been used in American schools: direct instruction and constructivist. In direct instruction, students are relatively passive in the learning process as the teacher does most of the talking while they sit quietly at their desks listening, responding when called upon, and completing assigned tasks. In contrast, a constructivist method focuses on inquiry based learning. Teachers guide and support students as they use existing knowledge to explore and uncover new information.

Regardless of what teaching method is used, increasing expectations and complexity occur as children become older.

The No Child Left Behind Act of 2001 is having a significant impact on shaping the school experiences of children in the United States. The act requires students to achieve grade level proficiency on standardized reading and mathematics examinations. If they do not perform adequately, school districts could face sanctions ranging from writing improvement plans that allow students to transfer within the school district to the state department of education determining if principals should maintain employment, teachers should receive pay raises, and if schools should stay open. This heavy emphasis on standardized test results cause many educators to feel boxed in as they are required to modify curriculum and instruction. For example, regardless of the age of the child, students are now expected to work silently and alone on seatwork that is clearly driven by skills that are measured on standardized achievement tests. This paper-and-pencil instructional strategy results in students spending many hours memorizing isolated facts that have little relevance to their everyday life. Many young people today simply perceive school as a series of tasks that need completion to advance to the next grade level; the joy of learning is absent. As the United States government has become increasingly involved in education, it also appears that the cognitive domain of human development is the main priority. A lack of emphasis on the development of the whole child has resulted in many students not being exposed to information regarding emotion and how certain feelings are often reflected in specific actions. A lack of emotional literacy may explain too why most behaviors appear to be based on instinct rather than intellect.

Changes in instructional practices have resulted from another educational trend: the inclusion movement. Students with a wide range of disabilities are now a part of the general education classroom. This relatively new educational approach often results in larger class sizes and vast learning differences between and among youth. To offset these challenges, special education professionals collaborate with regular education to design learning opportunities that are sensitive to all learners (Putman, 1993). Naturally, these ongoing fluctuations in school culture create a significant amount of anxiety and confusion among education professionals.

MEDIA

The media is influencing how individuals emotionally respond to stimuli simply due to the fact that children and adults are spending increasing amounts of time gaining information from a television, computer, or other electronic device. For instance, the Judge Baker Child Guidance Center in Boston indicated that children consume forty hours of media a week and twenty thousand commercials a year. The average child by the end of elementary school will witness eight thousand murders and one hundred thousand other acts of violence on television (Elkind, 2001). Levin (1998) also noted that 93 percent of boys and 78 percent of girls participate in video activities, commonly acting as perpetrators of aggression. In addition to entertainment violence, children are exposed to real-world trauma on television news. More than two-thirds of United States households view television reports of the gory details of the day's violence during dinner (Elkind, 2001). While most children cannot fully differentiate between what in the media is fantasy and what is real, some researchers have suggested that youth may become desensitized to violent behavior when they are repeatedly exposed to certain visual or auditory stimuli.

A number of emotion-based reasons have been provided to explain why people are spending increasing amounts of time viewing television or participating in computer activities. The most obvious is that some children and adults physiologically respond positively to certain visual and auditory stimuli presented in television shows, commercial advertisements, and movies. These mediums then naturally shape a variety of emotions and behaviors among people. For example, an exaggerated sense of fear seems to exist within society when media outlets replay isolated events such as school shootings and child abductions. Many individuals as well appear conditioned to believe that some events and specific actions happen everywhere at frequency levels that have never occurred before (Glassner, 1999). Other researchers have also suggested that the increase in technology usage is related to unsafe neighborhoods, and opportunities that were not previously possible. For instance, adults now have the ability to gain access to higher education through the Internet.

The media creates a sense of emotional uneasiness for some people. When individuals deviate from what is witnessed on television, they sometimes begin to question their identity and self-worth. Adults too seem to become confused when those portrayed in the media demonstrate increasing levels of extreme behavior. Examples of this are sometimes noticed in commercials that contain celebrities endorsing various products ranging from exercise regimens to long-term health insurance. The media also seems to create and perpetuate certain points of view through twenty-four-hour news stations, music videos, and reality television shows. Today, one perhaps can conclude with a high level of confidence that the media plays a significant role in shaping how individuals emotionally respond to certain environmental stimuli.

SUMMARY OF SOCIALIZING FORCES

Families, places of worship, schools, and the media provide information that acts as the emotional foundation for how individuals respond to certain environmental stimuli. Families today are thought to be different then they were a few decades ago. Increasing divorce rates, along with issues related to dating and remarriage, create a sense of emotional uneasiness for many family members. Places of worship as well consist of many emotion-based issues that at times create disharmony among societal members. Naturally, this ongoing sense of emotional discomfort is exacerbating and continues due the fact that schools do not teach emotional literacy. Rather, the focus in most United States schools is on finite skills that can be measured on a standardized test and the inclusion of students with disabilities in the regular education classroom. The media also relies on emotion to influence human behavior. For many children and adults, the media has created and perpetuated a culture of fear in order to shape certain thoughts and corresponding action.

WHY SOME PEOPLE HAVE THE ABILITY TO ADAPT THEIR BEHAVIOR AND OTHERS DO NOT

Human genetics plays a major role in determining if someone has the emotional aptitude to adapt their actions in response to environmental stimuli. Brazelton (1983) suggested that when a child is as early as two years old, adult care providers can identify patterns of emotion- based (temperament) behavior that determines future success or difficulties. For instance, if Billy is considered impulsive, he is more likely not to gain opportunities or acceptance from peers and adults. Levine (1994) also noted how differences in cognitive structure determine whether a particular person's brain is genetically limited or is highly specialized. Undoubtedly, some minds function very well in specific contexts or when confronted with certain demands but not under other circumstances. An example of this may be noticed when a student is trying to gain information from a librarian. The librarian may verbally explain an important concept for some individuals, and they will understand. Others, however, will need a visual image or tactile example to comprehend the information. A person's genetic endowment to some degree provides the emotional foundation to adapt to the many complexities within the environment.

Human genetics coupled with emotion often hinder a person's ability to think abstractly. This limitation causes some adults to function based on a primitive survival mentality regardless of their education or economic level. In many instances, they exhibit patterns of behavior to protect themselves similar to more primitive species. An example sometimes occurs when parents feel that their child is being punished at school for something they did not do. Some verbally argue with teachers and school administrators that their child was singled out and mistreated or how others are not telling the truth. Evidence of this type of behavior is also frequently witnessed at community organized youth baseball, football, and basketball games. As one would then expect, this survival mentality and model of protectionism often becomes indoctrinated into the behavioral repertoire of youth.

From a broader perspective, unintended outcomes sometimes result when emotion influences public policies and procedures. For instance, various labels and classification systems are often created in order to clarify issues of concern. This attempt to gain order is helpful to a certain degree; however, it oversimplifies information and may oppress certain groups of individuals. Many adults for example assume someone labeled as emotionally disturbed cannot function, and are dependent on family or others to live. In some cases, that is true but is not accurate for all those experiencing emotional difficulties. Another example frequently occurs when older members of society experience physical trauma. Social workers after certain types of surgeries usually rely on set protocols in an attempt to help the patient without talking and listening to their wishes. Not everyone in the same situation will need the identical kind of support. Patients are certainly not treated with dignity if they are placed in a predetermined category resulting in a longer more difficult time recovering from an invasive medical procedure. Another unintended emotion-based public policy outcome is the rate in which societal changes happen. It seems as though the phrase "This is how we do things here" reflects how emotion lessens the likelihood of change. For many individuals, the daily routines of life become predictable and safe resulting in a sense of contentment with the status quo. In other instances, it appears that tragedies have to happen such as someone having a heart attack or a country being under attack for individual and collective change to be considered. The emotions associated with concrete thinking as well seems to cause many adults to forget information if they are not directly involved or impacted by it in some way.

HUMAN BEHAVIOR: FEAR, SHAME, AND GUILT

The manner in which children and adults respond to environmental stimuli is often determined by the emotions of fear, shame, and guilt. These intense feelings distort reality and normally result in a response pattern in which someone has an experience, an emotion is generated, and if discomfort is present an action is emitted to lessen the uncomfortable feeling. An example of this may be found in a work environment. When a person is hired, an innate sense of uneasiness is present, causing the individual to experience anxiety as they speculate how their employer perceives them. These unsettling feelings for some adults result in over sensitivity and less productivity. However, a simple positive verbal comment or written note from a superior seems to increase the chance the employee will feel at ease and work productively. In other instances, if an employee has a history of negative work experiences or does not receive the level of psychological support needed, he will attempt to gain comfort from other things, such as talking to a coworker or participating in certain activities. These actions or routines sometimes become a way of life in order to gain a sense of personal safety. For others, certain coping mechanisms result in susceptibility to additional physical or emotional challenges. The emotions of fear, shame, and guilt may also explain why there are not clear behavioral norms and expectations for most activities of daily living.

The emotions of fear, shame, and guilt are having a tremendous impact on society. These feelings have the broad capability to alter every aspect of existence, from life expectancy to gross domestic product. More specifically, it appears that when adults spend a large amount of time in a state of emotional turmoil, they make poor decisions such as, consuming substances detrimental to their health, withdrawing from others who care about them or purchasing items they cannot afford. In many instances, an emotional spiraling effect results in poor health, few friends, and bankruptcy. When this happens, some adults seem to experience a level of discomfort and pain that parallels a physical fight that is perceived as never ending and impossible to win. This ongoing psychological struggle also naturally continues when parents model actions that communicate to their children how the world is out to harm them and that they should be on guard to protect themselves. Another example of the impact of fear, shame, and guilt is the War on Terror. After the events of September 11, 2001, many Americans seemed to demand a governmental response. They also seemed willing to do almost anything to feel safe. An example of this was observed at airports when travelers arrived hours ahead of time to wait in long lines while security officials examined their luggage. Even in remote locations, it was common to be told that you had to remove your shoes and jacket; otherwise, you would not be able to board the plane. It is clear that in spite of the many innate differences among children and adults related to fear, shame, and guilt, these emotions significantly influence behavior.

COMMON RESPONSES TO FEAR, SHAME, AND GUILT

People naturally react in a multitude of ways to fear, shame, and guilt. The most common response is to physically move away from whatever is causing the discomfort. Individuals during this period of time often contact others to avoid feeling afraid and isolated. For some, talking on the phone with a relative or visiting a friend seems to help them feel better. In other situations, if acute or persistent periods of fear are present, individuals avoid certain experiences such as venturing too far from their families. It is also evident that as adults participate in the activities of daily living, they develop psychological boundaries or walls to protect themselves from the discomfort and pain associated with fear, shame, and guilt. When these barriers are challenged, it too appears that a sensation of discomfort causes them to convey nonverbal and verbal messages to escape the situation. This communication pattern is sometimes observed when people lie or steal from others who trust them. Those who were harmed usually strengthen their boundaries in order to make sure no one emotionally hurts them again. Another example is sometimes noticed after someone has recently been divorced. In social situations, regardless of physical attraction, the emotionally hurting person usually communicates subtle messages that act to push the other person away as they are not ready to be emotionally vulnerable again. In some instances, it may take months or even years to process their past feelings. When they are ready, it may require large amounts of time to nurture the relationship; it may never be as fulfilling as it could have been because of previous psychological violations.

Comparing your life situation to others is another common response to fear, shame, and guilt. For example, the graphic images of violence in Bosnia or starvation in Ethiopia seems to distract attention from the realities of ones own life. Simply having knowledge of the experiences of those less fortunate seems to help individuals feel better. Statements such as "My life is not that bad. Look at those poor folks," and "Do you see how they are living?" make this point evident. In contrast, extensive media coverage of affluent lifestyles may result in greater emotional turmoil as individuals attempt to acquire something that is possibly unobtainable. It also appears that when a norm-referenced perspective on life is present, individuals develop a variety of rationalizations for their behavior. For instance, when adults are asked to do something they perceive as difficult, many state, "I can't do that. What will people think of me" or "It's just the way it is, and I cannot do anything about it." This typical pattern of behavior acts as a defense mechanism to buffer or distort the emotions generated from a given experience, thus allowing individuals to feel safe as they continue on in the activities of daily living.

Labeling and categorizing is another strategy used to lessen fear, shame, and guilt. It appears that when children and adults have knowledge of what something is they feel more safe and secure. An example of this occurs when someone visits their doctor to obtain a diagnosis and explanation for their condition. The information gained usually lessens their anxiety and helps them determine what they can do to feel better. Labeling and categorizing may help address feelings of fear, shame, and guilt; conversely, it could also be detrimental. When adults create images or stereotypes associated with certain groups, individuals are often oppressed. For example, adolescents who participate in gangs are often portrayed as hoodlums, criminals, and drug addicts even though many are not. These distorted perceptions may lessen the feelings of fear, shame, and guilt, but might also result in other unintended consequences.

CONSEQUENCES OF FEAR, SHAME AND GUILT

A number of consequences result from fear, shame, and guilt. The most obvious is that some adults have a general state of uneasiness permeating from them. This is evident when considering the number of individuals struggling with their health, personal relationships, and general outlook on life. In response to these uncomfortable feelings, many seem to be in an ongoing search for some form of control. Often, this need for a sense of power is reflected in someone's vocational identity. A possible example is an airline worker who feels as though their job is the only area where they have some level of control in life. In this situation, the employee may be unaware of how others perceive them as rude and disrespectful because they are constantly trying to protect their company position and false sense of authority. What is also interesting is how they sometimes respond when a traveler requests to speak to their supervisor; in many instances, their actions seem to reflect instinctive emotion-based behavior.

The emotions associated with a sense of lack of control may too explain why some adults seem to struggle with issues related to trust.

The emotions of fear, shame, and guilt affect the perception of time. For many individuals, there are simply not enough hours in a day to get everything finished. This sentiment causes some to state, "I just cannot get everything done no matter how hard I try" or "I do not even have enough time to catch my breath some days." When adults have these thoughts, they seem more prone to exhibit actions that reflect limited understanding of their emotions. This general sense of feeling constantly rushed, living in a whirlwind, also often contributes to poor decision making. An example is how increasing numbers of adults appear concerned with what other people think and value rather than determining for themselves what is important. This point is evident as many chose to take financial risks to obtain lavish homes and multiple automobiles in order to be perceived a certain way by others. Difficulties with the concept of time may too explain why individual and institutional change occurs at a very slow rate or does not happen at all.

A variety of other behaviors are exhibited in response to fear, shame, and guilt. The most obvious is harmful parenting styles. For instance, adults who use corporal punishment (spanking) often create a sense of fear in their children in order to avoid the shame they may feel if their child gets into trouble in the community. Others act as a friend rather then a parent in order to offset their guilt associated with divorce, poverty, or fear of the future. Additional outward signs of emotional discomfort might range from continually tapping a foot on the floor to tattooing multiple body parts. These variations in behavior patterns sometimes cause adults to wonder what is happening, as they cannot make sense of the actions around them. A recent example of this occurred after a college athletic team visited the United States Whitehouse. Many student athletes were perceived as disrespectful and poor reflections of their university because they wore flip-flop shoes, and did not wear jackets and ties. This sense of confusion and disillusionment regarding what is an appropriate and inappropriate actions result in many becoming judgmental and dependent on others to solve their problems. These feelings as well may explain why the government and other public institutions appear to be asked to assume more responsibility each year. Many other daily observations highlight the role of emotion in human behavior. However, rather than detailing more examples, one could possibly conclude that most, if not all, human actions are reflections of emotion more so than intellect.

CHAPTER SUMMARY

This chapter explored emotion and behavioral norms. It was suggested that emotion more so than intellect determines what is appropriate and inappropriate actions in certain contexts. Bandura's (1977, 1986) ideas were used as the theoretical foundation to consider how emotion is reflected in behavioral norms. A brief review of current trends in families, places of worship, schools, and media was conducted to illuminate how most actions represent the emotional state in which someone is experiencing at a particular point in time. It was also suggested that human genetics plays a significant role in determining if an individual has the emotional aptitude to adapt their actions in response to certain stimuli.

To conclude the chapter, the emotions of fear, shame, and guilt were presented as the underlying reason for most human actions. These feelings have the broad capability to alter every aspect of life ranging from life expectancy to the gross domestic product. More specifically, they typically result in a response pattern in which someone has an experience; if emotional discomfort is present, an action is emitted to lessen the uncomfortable feeling. Some of these instinctive and conditioned responses include physically moving away from whatever is causing the discomfort, talking on a phone with a friend or relative, or avoiding situations in the future that might result in fear, shame, and guilt. A number of consequences were then presented related to fear, shame, and guilt. The most obvious is that some adults have a general sense of uneasiness permeating from them. This emotional state seems to cause them to struggle with the perception of time. They as well often exhibit patterns of behavior that are detrimental not only to themselves but to others.

IDEAS TO PROMOTE BROAD SOCIETAL CHANGE

Life is easier today than in the past. Children and adults in most parts of the world no longer have to walk for miles to locate a river or stream to wash their clothes as water and electricity is readily available in most homes. Other innovations such as automobiles, refrigeration, microwave ovens, and computers have made daily experiences less physically demanding. In spite of these technological advancements, people still harm each other, certain groups cannot live in harmony resulting in wars that kill thousands, children continue to starve to death, and many adults are placed in prisons or other institutions in order to protect others in society. Why do these historical realities of the human experience continue? They persist today and will continue in the future because the core of human beings, emotion and intellect is impossible to significantly alter. Emotions more so than intellect also seems to determine what individuals ultimately hear, see, and do. With these thoughts in mind, the logical solution perhaps to societal problems is emotional self-awareness. This chapter, therefore, will attempt to provide a variety of observations and lifestyle considerations that might promote increased self-awareness. To begin, the role of emotion in everyday activities is once again discussed.

EMOTION

Human emotions are internal sensations that influence thought and behavior. Not all emotions though occur at the same rate, intensity level, or are perceived as having the same value. For example, innate survival instincts appear to cause negative emotions to overshadow positive. As these negative feelings surface, emotional discomfort usually triggers to some degree the autonomic nervous system. This biological-based response results in increased adrenalin, heart rate, and level of arousal. A recent example of this occurred when an athlete was running on a desolate dirt road. Despite traveling the same route for years, something different happened that day. While on mile number five, a group of dogs began chasing the runner. His body naturally responded by changing temperature, heart rate, and energy level in order to get away from the dogs. Of course, a pack of animals chasing someone is an extreme example; nevertheless, emotion-led behavior seems to be present everywhere. Emotions as well appear to act paradoxically; they help individuals feel safe, while simultaneously creating a sense of uneasiness.

Emotions create imprints on memory. Fear, the most primitive emotion, provides the answer as to why most adults seem to remember a sickness or family tribulation rather than a lovely play or concert. It too appears that the frequency and intensity of negative feelings determine the extent emotion-based memories hover slightly below consciousness. An example sometimes occurs when a person does not obtain a promotion or is terminated from their job. Despite many previous positive work experiences, the individual feels rejected as their ego and self-esteem is impacted. In response to what they perceive as unfairness or even injustice, the employee emotionally withdraws and remains in a state of disillusionment and pain for a certain period of time. This natural reaction causes many adults to avoid experiences that might result in emotional vulnerability. For some, no matter what happens, their life story contains a litany of examples of how they were mistreated and victimized by those around them.

Personal insecurities are more likely to arise when negative rather than positive emotions are recalled. Individuals in response to these unsettling feelings, typically develop a variety of coping strategies ranging from physical and emotional withdrawal, to remaining in a state of disillusionment. In between these two extremes, the time spent seeking comfort may lessen the probability individuals identify and obtain their hopes, dreams, and desires in life. From a broader perspective, when negative emotions outnumber positive, adults seem to struggle to trust those around them. This common way of thinking may explain why decisions are influenced more so by emotion rather than intellect. However, it spite of what might be perceived as obvious, broad societal change may have an increased chance of occurring if enough individuals gain a greater level of emotional self-awareness.

SELF-AWARENESS: THE LOGICAL ANSWER TO PROMOTE CHANGE

Self-awareness is thought of as understanding how one's emotion and intellect influence thoughts and actions. It is impossible obviously to be totally self-aware; yet, it may be possible to increase self-awareness. Adults who desire greater self-awareness are encouraged to prepare their spirit and mind prior to starting the journey. Some may want to observe the natural beauty of birds and the sky, interact with others whom they care about, or recall memories of pleasant times. As the path to increased self-awareness begins, many negative emotions will naturally surface. In spite of this, if you persist, a helpful strategy to lessen uncomfortable feelings is to try to emotionally remove yourself from the experience. It is as if you are physically present but are outside of yourself observing the events that are unfolding. For instance, when family members gather, observe the dynamic between individuals and the role you are playing at that particular point in time. How do you see yourself? Are you pleased with your behavior and the actions of those around you? If not, why not? This process may also provide valuable information to pinpoint the subtle variations in your emotions. It too may help you uncover that emotional discomfort and pain often reflects personal insecurities or aspects of life that are important to you.

As you continue on toward greater self-awareness, it might be helpful to consider a number of ideas. First, look within yourself rather than relying on external aspects to feel complete. Forget about the quest for something as it is "not greener or better on the other side of the street." Become a seeker of joy and tranquility (whatever that feels like and means to you) remembering that each experience is different because everything is in a constant state of transition. As an increased sense of self-awareness begins to occur, a state of calmness, acceptance, and hope may become present as never before, as you are becoming closer to harmony in spirit, mind, and body. When this happens, different and perhaps unusual thoughts might surface such as, "This is who I am, I am limited in many ways, but I have a passion to live life in a way that represents what is important to me." A simplistic but more tangible illustration might be associated with the concept of warts. Warts are physical blemishes that represent emotional violations that children and adults experience as they participate in the activities of daily living. These warts typically linger slightly below consciousness, often remaining the same size, becoming bigger or multiplying based on the length of time someone is in a state of emotional calmness or upheaval. It appears that as individuals identify and accept their psychological warts, they become more self-aware while simultaneously improving their general quality of life.

As one might expect, genetics provides the foundation for self-awareness. Each individual is endowed to some degree to have the ability to acquire and develop self-awareness skills. These genetic differences perhaps can be represented along a continuum beginning with little to extensive self-awareness. As children and adults interact with their environment, variables such as, parenting styles, school experiences, and a multitude of interactions within and between factors determine if they remain at the same point, regress or progress along their self-awareness continuum. At a more concrete level, genetic differences might explain why siblings significantly differ in their level of self-awareness in spite of having the same parents, sleeping in a room together, eating identical food, and sharing similar experiences as children. It is also important to remember that genetics plays a role in determining how people interpret and respond to certain contexts, sounds, textures, and colors and why motivation is a limited factor in developing certain skills. The limitations of motivation is sometimes noticed when teenagers want to increase their vertical leap to play basketball like their hero, LeBron James. Some will exercise extensively, lift weights, and change their diet. Despite their intense desire, genetics rather than effort will cause their vertical leap to only slightly increase. Others as well may have the ability to develop and use intricate motor movements needed for beautiful artwork but, at the same time they have difficulties exhibiting gross motor skills, such as running and jumping needed to participate in other leisure activities. After briefly considering how genetic endowment influences performance, it might be possible to suggest that the goal for each individual and society in general should not be something tangible but rather consist of an awareness of how emotion and intellect impacts certain thoughts and specific actions. Logically, if enough individuals obtain a higher level of self-awareness, increased chances of broad societal changes might result.

IDEAS THAT MIGHT RESULT IN INCREASED SELF-AWARENESS

In the following pages, five ideas will be presented for individuals to consider as they seek to gain increased self-awareness. At no time does the author believe the information is new or guarantees individual and collective change. However, regardless of how rational or absurd ideas seem, it is something to think about for those interested and concerned about not only their life but also the experiences of others.

IDEA ONE: INCREASE AWARENESS OF EMOTION

The first idea to consider in the process of gaining increased self-awareness is to identify and explore the complexities of your own emotions. Individuals need to understand and accept that certain environmental stimuli trigger biological based responses ranging from primitive reflexes to feelings labeled as joy, anger, happiness, love, hate, and a variety of other terms. These spontaneous and sometimes lingering sensations can be described along a continuum, beginning with innate reactions to scents, images and sounds, and ending with purposeful selection of stimuli. As children and adults coexist and interact with their environment, a natural approach and avoidance dichotomy seems to develop with certain stimuli generating pleasurable or troublesome emotions. This instinctive process of ongoing assessment and evaluation is shaped within the context of human genetics and positive reinforcement. An example perhaps is why some adults are attracted to particular individuals based on body shape, hair color, eyes, or way of thinking.

Once someone has a general understanding of primitive instinctive responses, it might be helpful to identify what sensations are commonly associated with the words happiness, sadness, anger, and guilt. Adults are encouraged to reflect upon a few life experiences in order to identify what aspects of a given situation result in the recall of certain emotions. For example, at a life-changing event such as a funeral, why is a certain comment remembered and not another? A variety of reasons such as, the psychological state of the person hearing the remark along with when and where it occurred might explain why it is recalled years later. A person's frame of reference is another variable to consider when thinking about emotions. Adults, due to the emotions associated with previous experiences, often seem to think that certain facts are the truth when they are not. This misconstruing of information may be reflected in the lingering emotions felt when individuals discuss historical accounts of war, prejudice, racism, and various other contemporary topics.

It is also important to remember that emotions in some instances are not easily identified or explained. It is as if they are innately present but do not appear as part of an ongoing thought. This emotional dullness or perceived lack of feeling varies for each individual; however, this aspect of the human experience can perhaps be illustrated through an automobile driving example. While traveling on a busy highway, a dog runs into the road and is hit by a car in front of you. The driver who hit the dog does not stop but rather continues to travel northbound despite knowing he has hit something. In this situation, how you and other witnesses respond highlight how emotions differ based on innate characteristics and personal values. Some for example might become angry with the driver or blame the dog for being in the road while others may have little concern for the driver or the pain experienced by the dog. In other instances, someone might become so emotionally upset with what had happened that they contact the police or are willing to spend large amounts of money to help the dog. When reflecting upon this example, it seems logical to suggest that individuals may become more sensitive to those around them when they are able to identify environmental triggers for certain emotions.

To further explore the complexities and subtleties of emotion, individuals are urged to examine the content of information they choose to include in their life. Discovering, for example, why some art forms are enjoyed and not others may be a beginning point to identify the nuances in emotion. Variations in color, shape, texture, pitch, volume, rhythm, and melody provide opportunities to discover why particular stimuli result in certain emotions and moods. Consideration should also be given to why various art forms are sometimes associated with specific experiences such as Queen's song, "We Are the Champions" played before and after an athletic event or a couple selecting a particular portrait reflecting their feelings toward each other. Television characters and movie story lines provide additional opportunities to explore why certain emotions surface. For many, this stimulus based self-assessment process creates a sense of empowerment in which individuals become more aware of their typical response to environmental stimuli.

In the end, adults are encouraged to identify aspects of life that create feelings of internal warmth. These sensations, frequently labeled as joy, result in increased energy levels, smiling, laughter, and a general feeling of calmness. Some educators for instance may experience joy when they sense a student has learned a skill. Businessmen who have high levels of productivity or gain significant profit from a venture might also obtain feelings of joy. It seems reasonable to suggest, that individuals would naturally increase their frequency of internal warmth (joy) when they uncover how their emotions impact their view of reality. As they gain this enhanced self-awareness, they too might notice aspects of their environment that have always been present but have gone unnoticed. For example, individuals' who willingly spend time observing their dogs tugging on a blanket together or experience the wonderful smells associated with walking along a beach or wilderness trail might have an increased sense of joy. It is also possible that collective feelings of joy can act as catalysts for change. If enough adults frequently experience internal warmth, they may be able to obtain the sense of emotional calmness needed to solve the many complex issues present in the world today.

Completing the worksheet activity found on the pages that follow may provide a more tangible means to increase your ongoing awareness of emotion.

IDEA TWO: TRADITIONS AND ASSUMPTIONS

Individuals should review the role of tradition in their daily lives. Traditions are established ways of thinking disseminated from one generation to the next. A simplistic example is names of people—such as Scott, David, and Tony representing males and Sally, Ann, and Beth signifying females. How did these designations develop and why are they so ingrained in the culture? Traditions in most instances derive from beliefs that are taught within a human indoctrination process consisting of family, places of worship, school, and media. Traditions as well provide the structure and predictability needed for children and adults to make sense of the world around them. Despite the many positive aspects of tradition, negative consequences sometimes result. The most obvious is that adults make assumptions about certain individuals, places, and things in order to simplify a particular term or issue of concern. An example in politics is the words *Democrat* and *Republican* . Is there a clear consensus as to what each of these terms mean and can someone demonstrate patterns of behavior labeled both Democrat and Republican? For most, assumptions act as protective barriers and reactions to feelings of anxiety, confusion, and disillusionment. It too appears that when a person believes information without much thought or question, they limit their potential as assumptions in many cases are inaccurate.

Traditions help people meet their innate need for safety. However, when challenged, individuals seem to become uncomfortable. This uneasiness is often reflected in the statement "This is how we have always done it." Another example is noticed in how adults react to someone new. Based on their outward characteristics and actions, they usually are accepted or are sent a variety of nonverbal and verbal messages to adapt their behavior. Additionally, hierarchal structures are less noticeable illustrations of how tradition affects human behavior. Institution organizational charts reflect individual and collective desires and beliefs for order and direction to obtain desired outcomes. The writing and implementation of various laws might also represent how adults react to violations of tradition. Traffic laws are the most obvious examples. Individuals are expected to drive a certain highway speed and change speed once in a city. Even within municipalities, adults are required to adapt their driving patterns based on the time of day and location.

Traditions are difficult to change because they are based more on emotion than intellect. For example, as a child's physical and emotional needs are met, they instinctively develop a sense of attachment to their care provider. This affectionate bond in most cases causes them to adopt their parents or guardians patterns of behavior. Of course, other variables such as siblings, extended family and friends, along with experiences in the neighborhood, school, and places of worship determine the extent in which tradition influences someone's ability for self-awareness. Another emotion-based variable to consider is when a tradition is questioned. Many adults seem to feel that they are rejecting their parents or disrespecting previous generations. This common way of thinking might explain why individuals often avoid discussing certain societal issues. It too may be the reason why some are unwilling to invest the energy needed to explore the many complexities associated with self-awareness. It also appears that most children and adults to some degree just want to be accepted within the existing framework of their family, vocation, and society in general.

More specifically, the initial step in determining how traditions influence daily behavior is to identify what aspects of life are important enough to spend time exploring. For some, it might be family, work, or friends. If family is chosen, a possible question to consider is, why is corporal punishment accepted in some households and not others? Tradition is the obvious answer as most adults appear to repeat child rearing practices similar to what they themselves experienced. When further questioned about this form of discipline, they also commonly state, "It worked for me as I turned out all right." In other situations, negative experiences cause adults to demonstrate behavior almost totally opposite of what they experienced. As individuals continue to review how traditions influence and shape daily life, they may gain the sense of empowerment needed to identify actions that are helpful and those that might be in need of altering or alleviating. As people ask, "Why are we doing this?" an opportunity exists as well to consider the purpose behind a certain action and possible alternatives which may result in more positive outcomes. Increased awareness of how traditions impact daily life may also help adults become more knowledgeable and sensitive to ways in which other cultures address topics of interest. This enhanced understanding coupled with ongoing reading may too result in the level of clarity needed to determine the role of tradition in the activities of daily living.

As the process of tradition analysis unfolds, adults seem to begin to rely on science more than emotion-based assumptions to guide their decision making. For this to continue though, children and adults need to develop the skills to comprehend information in order to understand explanations for given phenomenon. While reading, individuals are reminded that the truth regarding any aspect of life is often thought to be found somewhere in the middle of opposing viewpoints. For example, the recent discussion of global warming consists of various scientists sharing differing ideas. A level of accuracy surly exists in both lines of thinking;

however, further information is needed to explain global warming. At a more concrete level, adults are encouraged to monitor the frequency in which they make assumptions to guide their actions. For some, it might be helpful to write their daily experiences in a journal to chronicle how traditions shape their assumptions about life. Further understanding of tradition may also be gained by answering the following topic specific questions.

1. How do you determine if your physical appearance is

acceptable? What criteria guide the frequency in which you wash your hair or clothing? If you discussed this hygiene issue with one of your grandparents, would they have a different response?

2. In your family, do you meet each year at a certain person's home to celebrate the holiday season? Why does this occur and what variables might change this common pattern of behavior?

3. While at a place of worship, are rituals evident? How did they come about and why do people still participate in them?

4. Who or what determines public school education curriculum? Is all information taught perceived as equal? If not, how is specific content deemed more valuable?

5. In your place of employment, how is the institution organized? Does the structure reflect desired outcomes? If so, how does tradition influence how success is measured?

6. How are federal, state, and local traffic laws determined? Do they promote public safety or serve another purpose? Are there scientific studies explaining common driving patterns? If not, why are people punished for violating traffic laws?

IDEA NUMBER THREE: LESSEN CONCERN ABOUT WHAT OTHERS MIGHT THINK

A question to consider in the process of gaining increased self-awareness is why individuals are concerned about what other people think. The answer for most adults is that they have a desire to be liked and accepted by those around them in order to satisfy their need for a sense of belonging. Evidence of this common way of thinking appears to be present throughout time; however, recently it has become more noticeable. One possible reason is that the quality of life in industrialized countries has reached a level where most people have basic subsistence. As the standard of living increases, adults have more time and energy to spend on tasks other then providing food and shelter for their family. In spite of these significant changes in lifestyle, human emotions still create an atmosphere of comparison and competition among people. Another outcome of a higher standard of living is that many have not experienced a lack of something such as clean water or clothing. When this happens, children and adults seem to struggle determining the difference between what they need and want.

Completing the following questionnaire may provide helpful information to determine the emphasis you place on the perception of others. The lower the total number obtained, the greater the emphasis placed on the viewpoints of others.

DETERMINING THE EMPHASIS PLACED ON OTHER'S VIEWPOINTS QUESTIONNAIRE

Directions: Circle the number that reflects how you feel about each statement. The number key includes the following:

1=Always 2=Often 3=Sometimes 4=Seldom 5=Never

1. The experiences people have are determined by others.
12345

2. Life circumstances are based on individual actions.
12345

3. How someone is perceived by others is determined by physical appearance.
12345

4. The number and type of professional opportunities people receive are based on the clothes they wear.
12345

5. The cleanliness of a person's home is used to judge them.
12345

6. The type of car someone drives determines how others perceive them.
   12345

7. Gaining a particular job will affect happiness in life.
   12345

8. The ability to purchase the latest clothing styles determines how individuals perceive themselves.
   12345

9. The type and size of someone's home determines how others view them.
   12345

10. Adults view others as successful based on where they live.
    12345

11. Individuals in certain vocations are perceived more valuable than others.
    12345

12. People are in a quest for something in order to be happy.
    12345

13. What is considered appropriate behavior is determined by other people.
    12345

14. A person's selection of friends is based on a variety of variables.
    12345

15. Someone's friends will determine their status in life.
    12345

16. The amount and type of jewelry worn represents personal status.
12345

17. Participation in certain leisure activities indicates success.
12345

Now that you have completed the questionnaire, it is time to explore some of the possible consequences associated with being concerned about what others might think. In most situations, negative rather than positive outcomes seem to result. The most obvious detriment is that adults sacrifice some of their individuality when they attempt to be like those around them. They typically dress, think, and act in a certain way in order to be a part of a particular group. Once a member, they willingly accept and participate in a hierarchical structure where certain individuals are perceived more favorably than others. Terms such as *president, chief operating officer, superintendent, principal,* and *coach* make this point evident. It also appears that human emotion creates competition within any organization as individuals willingly conform in order to gain higher status. Belonging to a group certainly fulfills the need for acceptance; however, it also causes people to lose some of their individuality.

Being concerned about what other people might think may also be considered a form of self-oppression. For example, some individuals become lawyers, teachers, and doctors because of their parents' expectations when they would have rather been members of the military or work with animals. Adults who are concerned with how they are perceived by others are also more likely to adopt a norm-referenced life perspective in which they determine their identity and value in comparison to others. This point of view often causes them to search for a certain type of vocation or material possession to be perceived favorably. As this way of thinking unfolds and evolves, many seem to struggle with a lack of contentment and a sense of control in their life. In response to these uncomfortable feelings, adults usually demonstrate two patterns of behavior. One is to withdraw and become socially invisible. In this situation, psychological and social pressures force them to behave in ways that reflect a lack of hope and confidence. The second response is to engage in hyper-conformist social interactions. Individuals become members of one-dimensional group associating only with others who have similar ideas. Regardless of the coping strategy, it appears that at certain points in time in life almost all individuals are concerned about what others might think.

To lessen self-oppression, a specific strategy is needed to obtain a sense of empowerment and ultimately a higher level of self-awareness. The first step in this possibly life-altering process is to identify people that have significantly influenced you in some way. This may be your parents, relatives, friends, teachers, and others who you have shared experiences. From your list, select three to five whom you have a level of emotional intimacy and would like as a confidant. A confidant is someone that is a constant fixture in life supporting you in good and bad times. Contact each individual and thank them for previous experiences, stressing the positive role they have played in your life. Then ask them if they would agree to participate in a mutual confidant relationship. Once confidants are in place, as you experience daily events, place more emphasis on what they share rather than others. For example in a group situation, your confidant may point out that your verbal comments may have been misinterpreted. Adults are also encouraged to pay limited attention to what others say as they have little understanding of your intentions. Another strategy that might be helpful to lessen self-oppression is to decrease the amount of information gained from the media. Little attention should be given to commercial advertisements, network television characters, and story lines conveying personal success as a certain body image, home, jewelry, and type of automobile. In addition, adults should reflect upon the extent in which twenty-four -hour news stations influence how they perceive themselves and society in general. They too are encouraged not to believe that something is true just because it has been repeated a number of times. Often, these messages are myths and misinformation.

IDEA FOUR: ADOPTING A LEARNING OPPORTUNITY PERSONAL PERSPECTIVE

Individuals who adopt a learning opportunity personal perspective are more likely to increase their level of self-awareness. In any situation, information is available in which someone can gain knowledge of themselves and those around them. For example, even in the death of loved one, adults have the chance to explore how they felt about them, and are able to identify friends who provided comfort during this difficult period of time. As adults begin to change their thought process to a learning opportunity personal perspective, it would be remiss not to explore how socialization sometimes acts as a barrier to adopting this new way of thinking. Genetics coupled with the instinctive characteristics of human beings often result in children viewing the world much like those around them. For example, if teenagers are living in families not having a learning opportunity point of view, they themselves have less chance to adopt that perspective. Even while attending school, youth may not be exposed to a learning opportunity perspective because some educators do not promote intellectual curiosity and a joy of learning. Another possibly detrimental socialization variable occurs when families, schools, places of worship, and media present information as absolute truths. Relying on definitive answers to guide decision making is a reflection of emotion more so than a science-based learning opportunity personal perspective.

Communication skills are a vital component of a learning opportunity personal perspective. The ability to listen, pose questions, and understand nonverbal and verbal messages helps to gain information that may increase the general quality of life. Listening requires paying close attention to specific word choices without passing judgment or inserting your own opinion. To do this, children and adults should try to remain as calm and intellectually curious as possible in order to obtain the level of concentration needed to receive and interpret messages. Adults are also encouraged to monitor their use of verbal fillers to offset silence within a conversation. Despite these uncomfortable quiet moments, temporary pauses in dialogue may be beneficial as they allow opportunities to reflect on the emotions within certain thoughts. Individuals as well are urged to interact directly with others rather than relying on cell phones, e-mail, or other electronic devices to gain information. Technological advancements have increased the availability of information; yet, it appears that the depth of content knowledge has been sacrificed because individuals spend less time with each other discussing issues of concern. It is clear that a balance between the use of technology and human interaction is needed in order to develop the communication skills necessary to benefit from a learning opportunity personal perspective.

Documenting daily experiences is one strategy that might help individuals alter their current way of thinking. Those who participate in this activity will usually discover that an instinctive approach-avoidance dichotomy exists where certain labels and corresponding values are assigned that either increase or lessen participation. An example is sometimes noticed in the way in which some adults respond to others who have tattoos or body piercing. After the individual is noticed and visually scrutinized, a sense of comfort or uneasiness usually determines the quantity and quality of interaction between the two people. It further appears that when adults rely on emotion more so than intellect to govern actions, they lose opportunities to gain information that might increase their general quality of life. Children and adults therefore are encouraged to focus on observing the events that are occurring in their environment rather than evaluating them. A hypothetical automobile study might help to clarify this important change in perspective. Two researchers, over a five-day period, are spending three consecutive hours daily collecting data to determine the number of drivers traveling along a roadway and those wearing seatbelts. Results of the study indicate that 1,472 vehicles were observed and 1,223 drivers were wearing seatbelts. Someone with a learning opportunity personal perspective will not place a value on the findings but will simply report the facts. The following observation form might be another possible tool to consider in the process of adopting a learning opportunity personal perspective.

OBSERVATION FORM

Date	Activity Observed	Participants in Activity	Specific Behavior of Participants

Outcome of Those Interacting with Each Other or Their Environment	How Did You Feel About What Was Observed?	What Was Learned?	Based on what was learned, are their topics you are now curious about? If so, what are they?

Reflection is another important element of a learning opportunity personal perspective. It goes beyond mere impulsive and routine activity as it consists of reviewing an experience with serious consideration. An important component in this complex endeavor is to identify past experiences that shape current perspectives and specific actions. As events are identified, individuals are encouraged to accept and genuinely experience what is felt at a particular moment in time. An example is perhaps noticed in the behavior of Ms. Jones, a fourth-grade teacher. For approximately fifteen minutes each day, Ms. Jones creates a visual image of her students and the experiences she has had with each of them. She then focuses on determining how she feels about her verbal and nonverbal interactions. If she is unhappy with some of the exchanges, a plan can be developed consisting of specific strategies to nurture relationships. Reflection is a powerful way of thinking; however, adults should strive to have an intricate balance of positive and negative thoughts.

Another helpful reflective tool is a daily journal. Written records seem to provide a unique opportunity to document events in order to think about their personal and public meaning. This practice can also provide valuable insight to help adults understand why they might have certain thoughts and exhibit particular patterns of behavior.

As the process of adopting a learning opportunity personal perspective evolves, a number of consequences seem to result. Initially, an enhanced sense of calmness is present as individuals lessen and temper their impulsive responses to events that are happening around them. Adults as well appear to become more empowered rather than feeling overwhelmed by the trials and tribulations of daily events. This newfound sense of inner tranquility may possibly reflect a greater level of harmony between spirit, mind, and body. It too seems that while this change in perspective unfolds, adults begin to understand and appreciate the wisdom underlying statements such as "Once you leave your current job, you will be remembered as long as it takes for a ripple to settle after a rock has been dropped into a bucket of water," and "A job is really not that significant because you simply volunteer to work for an individual or institution for a period of time." The statement "We are all one" is another prolific phrase suggesting how we are all connected, sharing life together learning from each other. Ultimately, this new way of thinking will result in a belief and attitude that regardless of what might occur; it is a chance to learn.

In order to live life with a learning opportunity personal perspective, it is important to accept that some people will become uncomfortable in your presence because they are unable to comprehend your way of thinking. Their lack of understanding may trigger fear-based responses such as acts of anger and jealousy. Persevere, as this is another chance to learn about the emotional pain someone may be experiencing at a particular point in time. It is also recommended that you do not interpret hurtful comments literally; however, focus on the intensity in which they are conveyed as a measure of discomfort. Realizing and accepting that all behavior is communication will help you to be prepared for the emotional "push back" others might exhibit in response to your learning opportunity personal perspective.

IDEA FIVE: MEASURING SELF-AWARENESS

Now that specific strategies have been presented to increase self-awareness, it is time to consider how to measure it. A person's energy level is perhaps one way. It appears that the frequency and intensity of certain emotions often determine the amount of energy available to complete daily tasks. An example of this was observed at a college tennis match. All the athletes were talented; however, one player seemed to possess skills the others did not have. Despite his immense talents, he often became upset when missing what he thought was an easy shot. He would throw his racket to the ground and speak loudly in German. As the competition continued, he seemed to spend most of his time in a state of emotional upheaval. As a result, he lost both of his matches that day more than likely due to the energy spent on his frequent outbursts. When adults have limited self-awareness, like this tennis player, emotion more so than intellect may result in decisions that hinder performance and physical well-being. Another possible example is an employee who feels as though they have to work many hours to be perceived favorably, when in actuality that may not be true.

Changes in energy levels might also be reflected in the frequency and quality of multitasking. All individuals to a certain degree have the three main skills thought to be required for multitasking: memory, intellectual flexibility, and communication skills. Remembering prior actions is essential to create mental images and written lists to complete the activities of daily living. For example, if adults are able to recall when their employer reinforced them for outstanding productivity, they will exhibit similar behavior in the future. Intellectual flexibility is another skill necessary for multitasking. An individual's ability to adapt to different situations often determines if they can prioritize activities that need completing. It too appears that when adults accept that certain things just happen, such as a flat tire or a child becoming sick, they become more proficient in adjusting their thinking in order to multitask. The ability to communicate is also helpful in determining tasks that can be completed at the same time. Adults who communicate with a variety of individuals may gain the information needed to allocate the appropriate amount of energy to complete desired tasks.

When thinking about how emotion might impact memory, intellectual flexibility, and communication, it is helpful to observe and reflect upon specific events. For example, in the aftermath of Hurricane Ivan along the coast of Florida, many individuals struggled with the ability to multitask. Some appeared as though they were in a state of shock and depression while others became more insulated. Neighbors as well uncharacteristically began relying on each other as if they were old friends in spite of having limited contact prior to the tragic event. Many shoppers also appeared as if they were in a tunnel oblivious to what was happening around them. As they attempted to continue on in their activities of daily living, it seemed that the emotional trauma associated with the hurricane lingered for days, months, and perhaps years for some. Granted, hurricanes, states of depression, and self-insulation are extreme experiences and responses to life events; they are examples of how emotions affect the skills required to multitask. It is clear that regardless of what is occurring at a particular point in time, a certain level of emotional stress promotes or hinders the ability to multitask.

When adults rely on emotion more so than intellect to guide their actions, they often have difficulty deciding what activities can be multitasked. This lack of judgment has become so detrimental to state and local communities that legislation has been proposed to regulate citizen behavior. For instance, in some states, highway safety laws are being considered to punish those who text message while driving automobiles. Adults, at times, are even perceived by law enforcement as driving intoxicated when actually they are holding their cell phone on the steering wheel typing a text message. Multitasking is clearly not appropriate in certain situations. For instance, an engineer designing a building would increase the likelihood of error if they did not concentrate on one aspect at a time. Logically then, another way to measure self-awareness is a person's ability to determine tasks that can be completed at the same time.

As individuals contemplate tasks that can be completed simultaneously, they are urged to use an in-to-out perspective. This point of view suggests that the further away a task is from personal safety and relationships with others, the more likely it can be completed with another activity. For example, it would seem appropriate that someone could begin their laundry while talking on the telephone. Adults are encouraged to focus on activities they are participating in at the moment rather than allowing emotions to divert their thoughts. Emotion-based distractions clearly interfere with gaining accurate information and positive experiences. In order to obtain this intricate balance between completing activities and experiencing positive thoughts, adults are urged to write their life story and consider documenting their daily, weekly, or monthly experiences. When individuals record their thoughts, it might be possible to identify the extent in which emotion promotes or hinders the ability to multitask. Adults who maintain a journal may also uncover that most invasive thoughts are based on physical needs, the desire to be accepted, or some form of creativity. The following journal template might be helpful to determine how emotion impacts energy level and the ability to multitask.

JOURNAL TEMPLATE

Date:

Number of activities completed:

Respond to the following for each activity

    1. Activity (Describe if uncommon):

    2. Individuals participating in the activity:

    3. Emotions that surfaced during the activity:

    4. Were emotions uncommon (Circle: Yes or No)

    5. Specific behavior exhibited in response to emotions:

    6. Possible explanations for emotions and behavior exhibited:

    7. Did you complete other activities at the same time?

    8. Perceived outcome of the activity (explain):

    9. Amount of energy expended to complete activity:
       (Circle One: 1=large, 2=some, 3=little and 4=none)

CHAPTER SUMMARY

The purpose of this chapter was to provide ideas that might increase the chance of broad societal change. Self-awareness was presented as the only logical answer to promote change throughout the world. This theoretical construct was defined as one's ability to understand how emotion and intellect affect certain thoughts and specific actions. When adults explore how their emotions impact decisions, many perhaps will gain a sense of calmness, acceptance, and hope as they become closer to harmony in spirit, mind, and body. Ideally, a collective increase in self-awareness may generate the level of energy needed for change to occur.

Five ideas were then presented to increase self -awareness. The first was to identify and explore the complexities of emotion. Individuals were encouraged to recognize environmental stimuli that trigger biological based responses ranging from primitive reflexes to emotions labeled as joy, anger, happiness, love, hate, and a variety of other terms. Adults, while in the process of uncovering and understanding their emotions, were also urged to place special emphasis on identifying specific aspects of life that create feelings of joy. It was suggested that if enough people experience joy, they may obtain a sense of internal calmness required to collaborate with each other to solve complex issues of concern. The second idea explored the role of tradition in the activities of daily living. Traditions are ways of thinking disseminated from one generation to the next that provide children and adults with information to make sense of the world around them. Despite the many positive aspects of tradition, negative outcomes sometimes result such as, making assumptions about certain aspects of life. When an individual believes information without question, they may limit their potential as assumptions in most cases are inaccurate. To offset and possibly overcome the negative consequences associated with traditions, adults were urged to rely on science rather than intuitive thought to guide their actions.

The third and fourth ideas discussed ways of thinking. The third encouraged children and adults to lessen their concern with what others might think. Adults who worry about how they are perceived often adopt a norm-referenced life perspective in which they determine their identity and value in comparison to others. This point of view causes many to be in an ongoing search for something such as a certain type of vocation or material possession. Those embracing this lifestyle also seem overwhelmed and confused at times as to what might provide them a sense of empowerment, happiness, and contentment. Next, a learning opportunity personal perspective was discussed. This point of view consists of a belief and daily attitude that each experience is a chance to gain information that might improve the general quality of life. When individuals perceive life events as opportunities for growth, they seem more secure with their identity and become empowered rather than feeling overwhelmed by the trials and tribulations of daily events.

The final idea discussed how individuals could possibly measure self-awareness. A person's energy level was presented as a metric to calculate how emotion effects the completion of tasks. It was suggested that when adults rely on emotion more so than intellect to guide their actions, they naturally have limited energy available to multitask. Adults who struggle with the ability to multitask may also experience ongoing emotional difficulties as the demands of daily living become more complex. To offset these challenges, some ideas were provided related to determining tasks that could be completed simultaneously.

In the end, readers are encouraged to accept the fact that emotion is a wonderful aspect of the human experience. These sensations provide the foundation for who we are as individuals and society in general. All individuals would perhaps benefit if we allow the natural flow of energy associated with each emotion to occur rather than placing a predetermined term or value on what is felt. To nurture this change in thinking, it seems logical to suggest that we need to live in the moment rather than focusing on the past or future. Adopting this point of view may ultimately result in increasing numbers of adults gaining the level of self-awareness needed to understand how their emotion and intellect affect their thoughts and specific actions. Ideally, if enough people increase their self-awareness, broad societal changes might result.

REFERENCES

Arthur, J. (2003). *Education with character: The moral economy of schooling*. London, England: Routledge-Falmer.

Baldacci, L. (1991). 2-year report laments kid's moral climate. *Chicago Sun-Times, 30*, 24.

Bandura, A. (1977). *Social learning theory*. Englewood Cliffs, NJ:Prentice Hall.

Bandura, A. (1986). *Social foundations of thought and actions: A social cognitive theory*. Englewood Cliffs, NJ: Prentice Hall.

Baumrind, D. (1991). Parenting styles and adolescent development. In R. M. Lerner, A. C., Peterson, and J. Brooks-Gunn (Eds.), *Encyclopedia of adolescence*. New York, NY: Garland Publishing.

Becker, G. S. (1993). *Human capital: A theoretical and empirical analysis, with special reference to education* (3rd ed.). Chicago, IL: The University of Chicago Press.

Berk, L. E. (1998). *Development through the lifespan*. Boston, MA:Allyn and Bacon.

Binet. A., & Simon, T. (1916). *The development of intelligence in children*. Baltimore, MA: Williams & Wilkins. (Reprinted 1973, New York, NY: Arno Press; 1983, Salem, NH: Ayer Company).

Brazelton, T. B. (1983). *Infants and mothers: Differences in development* (Rev. ed.). New York, NY: Dell.

Broecker, W. (1975). Climatic change: Are we on the brink of a pronounced global warming? *Science, 189,* 460–463.

Bronfenbrenner, U. (1979). *The ecology of human development: Experiments by nature and design.* Cambridge, MA: Harvard University Press.

Bronfenbrenner, U. (1995). The bioecological model from a life course perspective: Reflections of a participant observer. In P. Moen, G. H. Elder Jr., and K. Luscher (Eds.), *Examining lives in context* (pp. 599–618). Washington, DC: American Psychological Association.

Bronfenbrenner, U. (1997). *The ecology of developmental processes.* In R. M. Lerne (Ed.), *Handbook of child psychology: Theoretical models of human development.* New York, NY: Wiley.

Caring. (2009). Merriam-Webster Online Dictionary. Retrieved from http://www.merriamwebster.com/dictionary/caring

Diamond, J. (1997). *Guns, germs, and steel: The fates of human societies.* New York, NY: W. W. Norton & Company.

Elkind, D. (2001). *Hurried child: Growing up too fast too soon* (3rded.). Cambridge, MA: Perseus Book Group.

Erikson, E. H. (1968). *Identity: Youth and crisis.* New York, NY:W. W. Norton & Company.

Farr, J., Hacker, J. S., and Kazee, N. (2006). The policy scientist of democracy: The discipline of Harold D. Lasswell. *American Political Science Review, 100*(4), 579–587.

Federal Interagency Forum on Child and Family Statistics (2004). *America's children in brief: Key national indicators of well-being,* Washington, DC.

Firth, U. (1991). *Autism and Asperger Syndrome* (translated and annotated version of Asperger's 1944 paper),

Cambridge, England: University Press.

Freud, S. (1938). *An outline of psychoanalysis*. London, England: Hogarth.

Furstenberg, F. F., and Nord, C. W. (1985). Parenting apart: Patterns of childrearing after marital disruption. *Journal of Marriage and the Family, 47*, 893–904.

Glassner, B. (1999). *The culture of fear: Why Americans are afraid of the wrong things*. New York, NY: Basic Books.

Grygier, T. (1954). *Oppression: A study in social and criminal psychology*. London, England: Routledge & Kegan Paul Ltd.

Halpren, D. (2004). Social capital. Hoboken, NJ: John Wiley and Sons.

Hambrick, D. Z. and Engle, R. W. (2003). The role of working memory in problem solving. In J. E. Davidson & R. J. Stenberg (Eds.). *The psychology of problem solving* (pp. 176–205). Cambridge, England: Cambridge University Press.

Hardman, M. L., Drew, C. J., and Egan, M. W. (2006). *Human exceptionality: School, community, and family*. Boston, MA: Allyn & Bacon.

Harrub, B., Thompson, B., and Miller, D. (2003). The origin of language and communication. *Journal of Creation, 17*(3), 93–101.

Hersey, P., and Blanchard, K. H. (1988). *Management of organizational behavior: Utilizing human resources*. Englewood Cliffs, NJ: Prentice Hall.

Insel, P. M. and Roth, W. T. (1990). Core concepts in health (8th ed.). Mountain View, CA: Mayfield.

Jerden, L. (1995). *A world of oppression: Plight of women*. Lake Forest, CA: Assist News Services.

Johnson, B. (2010). AP survey: Most Alabama legislators favor bill to ban sending text messages while driving. *Dothan*

Eagle, January 6, 2010.

Johnston, J. R., Kline, M., and Tschann, J. M. (1989). Ongoing post-divorce conflict. *American Journal of Orthopsychiatry,59*, 576-592.

Kessler, D. B. and Dawson, P. (1999). *Failure to thrive and pediatric under nutrition: A transdisciplinary approach.* Baltimore, MA: Paul H. Brookes Publishing.

Khaldun, I. (2005). *The Muquaddimah: An introduction to history.* Princeton, NJ: Princeton University Press.

Kingdon, J. W. (1984). *Agendas, alternatives, and public policies.* Boston, MA: Little, Brown and Company.

Kochanska, G., Casey, R. J., and Fukumoto, A (1995). Toddlers' sensitivity to standard violations. *Child Development, 66,* 643–656.

Kohlberg, L. (1969). Stage and sequence: The cognitive-developmental approach to socialization. In D. A. Goslin (Ed.), *Handbook of socialization theory and research.* Chicago, IL: Rand McNally.

Kozol, J. (1991). *Savage inequalities: Children in America's schools.* New York, NY: Crown.

Kubler-Ross, E. (1969). *On death and dying.* New York, NY: McMillian.

Lasswell, H. D. (1958). *Politics: Who gets what, when, and how?* Cleveland, OH: The World Publishing Company.

Lasswell, H. D. (1965). *World politics and personal insecurity.* New York, NY: The Free Press.

Lasswell, H. D. (1971). *A preview of policy sciences.* New York, NY: American Elsevier.

Lebech, M. (2004). What is human dignity? *Maynooth Philosophical Papers*, 59–69.

Levin, D. E. (1998). *Remote control childhood? Combating the hazards of media culture.* Washington, DC: National

Association for the Education of Young Children.

Levine, M. D. (1994). *Educational care: A system for understanding and helping children with learning problems at home and in school.* Cambridge, MA: Educators Publishing Services, Inc.

Locke, J. (1690). *An essay concerning human understanding.* Indianapolis, IN: Hackett Publishing Company.

Maslow, A. H. (1943). A theory of human motivation. *Psychological Review, 50* (4), 370–396.

Maslow, A. H. (1968). *Toward a psychology of being* (2nd ed.). Princeton, NJ: Van Nostrand.

Maslow, A. H. (1971). *The farther reaches of human nature.* New York, NY: The Viking Press.

Maslow, A. H. (1987). *Motivation and personality* (3rd ed.). New York, NY: Harper & Row.

McLaren, B. (2004). *A generous orthodoxy: Why I am a missional, evangelical, post/Protestant, liberal/conservative, mystical/poetic, biblical, charismatic/contemplative, Fundamentalist/Calvinist, Anabaptist/Anglican, Methodist, Catholic, Green, incarnational, depressed-yet -hopeful, emergent unfinished Christian.* Grand Rapids, MI: Youth Specialties Books.

McWhorter, J. (1998). *The word on the street: The fact and fable about American English.* New York, NY: Plenum Trade.

McWhorter, J. (2003) . *Doing our own thing: The degradation of language and music and why we should, like, care.* New York, NY: Gotham.

Meyer. D. R., and Garasky, S. (1993) . Custodial fathers: Myths, realities, and child support policy. *Journal of Marriage and the Family, 55,* 73–79.

Moisi, D. (2009). *The geopolitics of emotion: How cultures of fear, humiliation, and hope are shaping the world.* New York, NY: Doubleday.

Moreno, R. (2006). Learning in high-tech and multimedia environments. *Current Directions in Psychological Science,* 15(2), 63–67.

National Center for Education Statistics (2004). *Paying for college: Changes between 1990 and 2000 for full-time dependent undergraduates.* Washington, DC: US Department of Education.

National Commission on Excellence in Education (1983). *A nation at risk: The imperative for educational reform.* Washington, DC: United States Department of Education.

No Child Left Behind Act of 2001, Pub. L. No. 107–110, 115 Stat. 1425 (2002).

Olasky, M. (1992) . *The tragedy of American compassion.* Washington, DC: Regency Publishing Inc.

Pelham, B (2009). *Awareness, opinions about global warming vary worldwide.* Washington, DC: The Gallup Organization.

Piaget, J. (1930). *The child's conception of the world.* New York, NY Harcourt, Brace & World.

Piaget, J. (1937). *The construction of reality in the child.* New York, NY: Basic Books.

Piaget, J. (1952). *The origins of intelligence in children.* New York, NY: International Universities Press.

Pinker, S. (1995). *The language instinct.* New York, NY: Harper Perennial.

Pinker, S. (2002). *The blank slate: The modern denial of human nature.* New York, NY: Penguin Putnam Inc.

Pinker, S. (2007). *The stuff of thought: Language as a window into human nature.* New York, NY: Penguin Putnam Group.

Podgorecki, A. (1993). *Social oppression.* London, England: Greenwood Press.

Pogrebin, L. C. (1983). *Family politics*. New York, NY: McGraw-Hill.

Postman, N. (1985). *Amusing ourselves to death: Public discourse in the age of show business*. New York, NY: Penguin Books.

Putnam, J. W. (1993). *Cooperative learning and strategies for inclusion: Celebrating diversity in the classroom*. Baltimore, MA: Brookes Publishing.

Regoli, R. M. and Hewitt, J. D. (1994). *Delinquency in society (2*nd ed.*)*. New York, NY: McGraw-Hill.

Sachs, J. D. (2008). *Common wealth: Economics for a crowded planet*. New York, NY: Penguin Press.

Schor, I. (1992). *Empowering education: Critical teaching for social change*. Chicago, IL: The University of Chicago Press.

Schunk, D. H. (2004). *Learning theories: An educational perspective* (4th ed.) . Upper Saddle River, NJ: Merrill Prentice Hall.

Searleman, A. and Herrmann, D. (1994). *Memory from a broader perspective*. New York, NY: McGraw-Hill.

Siegel, D. J. (1999). *The developing mind: Toward a neurobiology of interpersonal experience*. New York, NY: Guilford.

Skinner, B. F. (1983). *A matter of consequences*. New York, NY: Knopf.

Skinner, B. F. (1984). The shame of American education. *American Psychologist, 39* (9), 947–954.

Skinner, E. A. and Belmont, M. J. (1993). Motivation in the classroom: Reciprocal effects of teacher behavior and student engagement across the school year. *Journal of Educational Psychology, 85*, 571–581.

Smith, A. (1991). *Wealth of nations*. Amherst, NY:

Prometheus Books.

Snook, I. A. (1972), *Concepts of Indoctrination*. London, England: Routledge & Kegan Paul.

Snowman, J., McCown, R., and Biehler, R. (2009). *Psychology applied to teaching* (12th ed.). Boston, MA: Houghton Mifflin Company.

Stainback, S., Stainback, W., and Forest, M. (Eds.) (1989). *Educating all students in the mainstream of regular education*. Baltimore, MA: Brookes Publishing.

Sullivan, A. and Sheffrin, S. M. (2003). *Economics: Principles in action*. Upper Saddle River, NJ: Pearson Prentice Hall.

Tanner, L. (2006). Survey: 17 percent at two Ivy League schools practice cutting, other self-abuse. *Dothan Eagle*, June 5, 2006.

Turnbull, A. P., Turnbull, H. R., Shank, M., and Leal, D. (2010). *Exceptional lives: Special education in today's school* (6th ed.). Upper Saddle River, NJ: Prentice Hall.

Universal Declaration of Human Rights, G. A. res. 217A (III), U.N. Doc A/810 at 71 (1948).

Watson, J. (1985). *Nursing: The philosophy and science of caring*. Niwot, CO: University Press of Colorado.

Watson, J. (1999). *Postmodern nursing and beyond*. Toronto, CA: Churchill Livingstone.

Webster's Desk Dictionary (1993). New York, NY: Gramercy Books.

Werner, U. (2002) . Public policy analysis, in Daellenbach, H. G. and Flood, R. L. *The informed student guide to management science*. London, England: Thomson Learning.

Whitbourne, S. K. (1996). *The aging individual: Physical and psychological perspectives*. New York, NY: Springer.

Woolcock, M. (2001). The place of social capital in understanding social and economic outcomes. *Canadian*

Journal of Policy Research 2(1) 1–17.
Young, I. (1990). *Justice and the politics of difference.* Princeton, NJ: Princeton University Press.

www.ingramcontent.com/pod-product-compliance
Lightning Source LLC
Chambersburg PA
CBHW071430070526
44578CB00001B/58